INTRODUCING
ISSUES WITH
OPPOSING
VIEWPOINTS®

Television

Other books in the Introducing Issues
with Opposing Viewpoints series:

AIDS
Civil Liberties
Cloning
The Death Penalty
Gangs
Gay Marriage
Genetic Engineering
Smoking
Terrorism

INTRODUCING
ISSUES WITH
OPPOSING
VIEWPOINTS®

Television

Emma Bernay, *Book Editor*

Christine Nasso, *Publisher*
Elizabeth Des Chenes, *Managing Editor*

GREENHAVEN PRESS
A part of Gale, Cengage Learning

GALE
CENGAGE Learning™

Detroit • New York • San Francisco • New Haven, Conn • Waterville, Maine • London

For more information, contact
Greenhaven Press
27500 Drake Rd.
Farmington Hills, MI 48331-3535
Or you can visit our Internet site at gale.cengage.com

LIBRARY OF CONGRESS CATALOGING-IN-PUBLICATION DATA

Television / Emma Bernay, book editor.
    p. cm. — (Introducing issues with opposing viewpoints)
    Includes bibliographical references and index.
    ISBN-13: 978-0-7377-3853-7 (hardcover)
    1. Television programs—United States.   2. Television and children.   3. Television
broadcasting.   I. Bernay, Emma.
    PN1992.3.U5T367 2007
    791.450973—dc22
                                                                    2007030380

ISBN-10: 0-7377-3853-7 (hardcover)

Printed in the United States of America
 2 3 4 5 6 7 12 11 10 09 08

Contents

Foreword   7

Introduction   9

Chapter 1: Is Television Harmful?

1. Television Is Harmful   13
   Ann Vorisek White
2. Television Is Not Always Harmful   20
   Anna Quindlen
3. Television Contributes to Childhood Obesity   25
   Steven Gortmaker
4. Television Ads Are Not Necessarily Responsible for Obesity   30
   Douglas J. Wood

Chapter 2: What Is Society's Relationship to Television?

1. Television Content Should Be Censored   37
   Tony Perkins
2. Television Content Should Not Be Censored   42
   Jacob Sullum
3. Television Leads to Moral Decline   47
   Brian Fitzpatrick
4. Television Does Not Lead to Moral Decline   52
   Ronald Bailey
5. Reality TV Has Positive Qualities   58
   Ian Wilhelm
6. "Reality" Television Does Not Have Positive Qualities   68
   Howard Rosenberg

Chapter 3: Who Should Control Television?

1. Networks Should Take Responsibility for Harmful Television
   Content   74
   Michael Tracey
2. Parents Should Take Responsibility for Harmful
   Television Content   79
   Adam Thierer

3. Cable Channel Choice Should Be Permitted   86
   Martha Kleder
4. Cable Channel Choice Should Not Be Permitted   92
   David L. Cohen

Facts About Television   97
Glossary   100
Organizations to Contact   101
For Further Reading   107
Index   113
Picture Credits   119

Indulging in a wide spectrum of ideas, beliefs, and perspectives is a critical cornerstone of democracy. After all, it is often debates over differences of opinion, such as whether to legalize abortion, how to treat prisoners, or when to enact the death penalty that shape our society and drive it forward. Such diversity of thought is frequently regarded as the hallmark of a healthy and civilized culture. As the Reverend Clifford Schutjer of the First Congregational Church in Mansfield, Ohio, declared in a 2001 sermon, "Surrounding oneself with only like-minded people, restricting what we listen to or read only to what we find agreeable is irresponsible. Refusing to entertain doubts once we make up our minds is a subtle but deadly form of arrogance." With this advice in mind, Introducing Issues with Opposing Viewpoints books aim to open readers' minds to the critically divergent views that comprise our world's most important debates.

Introducing Issues with Opposing Viewpoints simplifies for students the enormous and often overwhelming mass of material now available via print and electronic media. Collected in every volume is an array of opinions that capture the essence of a particular controversy or topic. Introducing Issues with Opposing Viewpoints books embody the spirit of nineteenth-century journalist Charles A. Dana's axiom: "Fight for your opinions, but do not believe that they contain the whole truth, or the only truth." Absorbing such contrasting opinions teaches students to analyze the strength of an argument and compare it to its opposition. From this process readers can inform and strengthen their own opinions, or be exposed to new information that will change their minds. Introducing Issues with Opposing Viewpoints is a mosaic of different voices. The authors are statesmen, pundits, academics, journalists, corporations, and ordinary people who have felt compelled to share their experiences and ideas in a public forum. Their words have been collected from newspapers, journals, books, speeches, interviews, and the Internet, the fastest growing body of opinionated material in the world.

Introducing Issues with Opposing Viewpoints shares many of the well-known features of its critically acclaimed parent series, Opposing Viewpoints. The articles are presented in a pro/con format, allowing readers to absorb divergent perspectives side by side. Active reading questions preface each viewpoint, requiring the student to approach the material thoughtfully and carefully. Useful charts, graphs, and cartoons supplement each article. A thorough introduction provides readers with crucial background on an issue. An annotated bibliography points the reader toward articles, books, and Web sites that contain additional information on the topic. An appendix of organizations to contact contains a wide variety of charities, nonprofit organizations, political groups, and private enterprises that each hold a position on the issue at hand. Finally, a comprehensive index allows readers to locate content quickly and efficiently.

Introducing Issues with Opposing Viewpoints is also significantly different from Opposing Viewpoints. As the series title implies, its presentation will help introduce students to the concept of opposing viewpoints, and learn to use this material to aid in critical writing and debate. The series' four-color, accessible format makes the books attractive and inviting to readers of all levels. In addition, each viewpoint has been carefully edited to maximize a reader's understanding of the content. Short but thorough viewpoints capture the essence of an argument. A substantial, thought-provoking essay question placed at the end of each viewpoint asks the student to further investigate the issues raised in the viewpoint, compare and contrast two authors' arguments, or consider how one might go about forming an opinion on the topic at hand. Each viewpoint contains sidebars that include at-a-glance information and handy statistics. A Facts About section located in the back of the book further supplies students with relevant facts and figures.

Following in the tradition of the Opposing Viewpoints series, Greenhaven Press continues to provide readers with invaluable exposure to the controversial issues that shape our world. As John Stuart Mill once wrote: "The only way in which a human being can make some approach to knowing the whole of a subject is by hearing what can be said about it by persons of every variety of opinion and studying all modes in which it can be looked at by every character of mind. No wise man ever acquired his wisdom in any mode but this." It is to this principle that Introducing Issues with Opposing Viewpoints books are dedicated.

Introduction

"Television is like a beloved relative who came to live with us. At first he keeps himself up, bathes regularly and regales us with rollicking adventures of his adventurefilled [sic] life. But in time his evening nip of sherry becomes all-day tippling. The rollicking tales become bawdy and then obscene."

Omaha World-Herald, editorial, May 16, 2005.

The topic of television has been a source of almost constant public debate since Americans first began watching television in their homes in the 1950s. TV carries the distinction of being a medium that is both popular and maligned. It has been called "the idiot box" and the "boob tube;" at the same time, TV has carried news and views of the world to millions of people who would not otherwise have access to them.

Americans discuss the merits and harms of television-watching, yet adults consume three to four hours of TV a day. Parents and experts generally agree that excessive television watching is harmful to children, but 70 percent of children have a television in their bedrooms and spend an average of four hours a day watching. Despite the communications revolution brought on by the Internet, television's influence on society has remained undiminished, as has the controversy surrounding it.

The controversy around television tends to center around the danger of harmful content versus the relative harm of excessive government regulation. The increasing prevalence of violent and sexual situations on network television shows has alarmed many family-values advocacy groups and media watchdog organizations as well as some child-care experts. These groups have called on the Federal Communications Commission (FCC) and on the industry itself to restrict harmful content. Yet free-speech advocates, libertarian groups, and industry representatives argue that regulation must be minimal and limited; greater governmental controls tread into the area of censorship and violations of constitutionally guaranteed rights.

The debate over harmful content versus governmental control has at its core a simple question: who owns television? Family-values and media awareness groups tend to believe that the viewers are the owners of television; they are the consumers and should decide what is broadcast. These groups include the American Decency Association and the Media Awareness Network, among others. In testimony before Congress, L. Brent Bozell, head of the media watchdog Parents Television Council, stated:

> [The] vast majority of Americans [are] sick and tired of the sewage pouring out of their airwaves, or on cable programs they are being forced to underwrite. . . . [The] broadcast airwaves are public property. They belong to the people. All the people. Broadcasters are given a license—a temporary right—to use this public property in exchange for a promise to serve the public interest.[1]

The viewers have the right to call on their democratic government to regulate television content, if they so choose.

Others disagree with this reasoning; industry groups, free-speech and libertarian groups such as TV Watch, the Cato Institute, and the First Amendment Center argue that the industry owns television. Increasing government regulation to combat the surge in violence and sex on TV infringes on civil liberties. Rather, they argue, consumers should simply not watch shows they find offensive or should boycott networks to register their alarm. First Amendment Center director Ken Paulson emphasizes the importance of broadcast autonomy in a discussion of a sexual incident accidentally broadcast on television: "[The incident] lays bare the unique nature of America's broadcasters—media companies that are licensed by the government, but also enjoy First Amendment protection. . . . In a nation in which our most immediate and powerful medium is television, we can't turn content regulation over to a handful of political appointees in Washington."[2]

Congress has entered the debate in recent years; in 2006, the House passed and President George W. Bush signed into law legislation that increases the amount of fines the FCC can levy for broadcast inde-

---

[1] L. Brent Bozell, "Testimony Before the U.S. Senate Committee on Commerce, Science, and Transportation on Indecency," January 19, 2005.
[2] Ken Paulson, "Flashpoint: Janet Jackson and Government Regulation of TV," First Amendment Center, February 6, 2004.

cency. Previously, the maximum amount the FCC could fine a station was $32,500. The Broadcast Indecency Enforcement Act increased the figure tenfold, to $325,000. This tips the balance of power in favor of the government: The punishment they can mete out to broadcasters is given more clout. The National Association of Broadcasters (NAB), an industry trade group, disagreed with the increased fines and in a statement reinforced the idea that the industry owns television and consumers must police themselves. Responding to the passage of the bill, the association said, "In issues related to programming content, NAB believes responsible self-regulation is preferable to government regulation."[3]

Other issues can intensify the debate. Parents and media-awareness groups have accused the food industry of worsening the childhood obesity problem by specifically targeting children in commercials for junk food. Advertisers insist that parents need to resist buying junk food and turn off the TV if they are unhappy with content. Parents and child-health advocates argue that both advertisers and the broadcast industry must restrict commercials aimed at children—and if they refuse to do so voluntarily, some say, the government must force them to do so.

On the other hand, the industry has pointed out that if they own television and control it, they can highlight aspects of American society that might be otherwise overlooked. In cable subscriptions, for instance, that consumers must buy in packages, the industry can offer small channels highlighting African American or Hispanic issues. If consumers were allowed to pick and choose which cable channels they want to subscribe to, as many conservative family-values groups have suggested should happen, these smaller channels would quickly die.

Ninety-nine percent of American households have at least one television. The medium is pervasive and important—unlike many other controversial issues, television affects virtually all of American society. The images broadcast into people's living rooms are created by executives far away. The issue of who owns television and who should control it—the consumers, the industry, or the government—is far from resolved. *Introducing Issues with Opposing Viewpoints: Television* will explore this debate and its various aspects.

---

[3] Tom Henry, "Bush Signs Bill to Increase FCC Indecency Fines," *Jurist*, June 15, 2006.

Chapter 1

Is Television Harmful?

People's concerns about the harm of television often center on its effects on children.

Television Is Harmful

Ann Vorisek White

In this viewpoint, Ann Vorisek White claims that television viewing is harmful to children and families. She explains that families are no longer spending the necessary time to bond and teach their children because of excessive television time. According to White, children are exposed to more and more violence on TV, and their behavior is negatively reflecting that exposure. Language and imagination are stifled, White argues, since television does not provide children with the means to develop these skills. Ann Vorisek White is a children's librarian and has a master's degree in library science.

"As a result of the many hours they spend in front of the TV, children are in effect being parented by network producers rather than by their own parents."

AS YOU READ, CONSIDER THE FOLLOWING QUESTIONS:
1. According to the author, during what years does the brain develop most?
2. How does television stifle conversation and teach children to be passive and unquestioning viewers, according to White?
3. What does White suggest one does to fill the time that would have been spent watching TV?

The average American child watches four hours of television every day, according to the American Academy of Pediatrics. Videotapes and video games add to the amount of time children spend staring at a screen. How does all this viewing affect us?

Television harms our children and families in many ways. Before TV, meals were a time for families to reflect upon the day and linger in peace or lively discussion over home-cooked meals. Today, most American families regularly watch television during dinner.

Mealtimes are hurried, with children and adults eating in silence, eyes glued to the screen, or gobbling down their food in order to return to the family room to resume their interrupted television watching.

Loss of Family Bonding

Childhood illnesses and injuries leading to bed rest used to be special times for bonding and family rituals. We can recall books that were read to us or quiet games that we played while recovering from chicken pox or a broken leg. Today, sick children spend their days watching videos and television.

Some people believe that cutting back on television watching brings families closer together.

In the past, holiday gatherings found children playing outdoors and adults gathered in lively discussions. Today, children are more apt to gather around the television or computer than to take up a game of kick-the-can or capture-the-flag. In fact, some family gatherings seem to revolve around TV, with Thanksgiving dinners prepared to suit the timing of football games.

As a result of the many hours they spend in front of the TV, children are in effect being parented by network producers rather than by their own parents. Television teaches children that rude, irresponsible behavior is not only acceptable but also glamorous. Children learn about sex and violence apart from their consequences, emotional attachments, and responsibilities. They learn to act impulsively, without reflection or advice from elders. Qualities such as wisdom and processes like thinking through a problem are difficult to express on a television screen, especially when the medium depends on sensationalism and shock rather than character and insight.

TV Violence Shapes Children

US Surgeon General David Satcher stated in a 2000 report on youth violence that violent television programming and video games have become a public-health issue and that "repeated exposure to violent entertainment during early childhood causes more aggressive behavior throughout a child's life. The American Psychological Association (APA) notes that children who regularly watch violence on television are more fearful and distrustful of the world, less bothered by violence, and slower to intervene or call for help when they see fighting or destructive behavior. A Los Angeles Times story reported that 91 percent of children polled said they felt "upset" or "scared" by violence on television. A University of Pennsylvania study found that children's TV shows contain roughly 20 acts of violence each hour. After watching violent programs, the APA reports, children are more likely to act out aggressively, and children who are regularly exposed to violent programming show a greater tendency toward hitting, arguing, leaving tasks unfinished, and impatience. The first two years of life is when the greatest and most rapid development of the brain occurs. As all parents know, a child's mind is different from an adult's, and the differences go beyond children's innocent and often poetic perceptions of the world. While the adult brain has two distinct hemispheres, the infant brain is a single receptacle of sensory experience in which neither side has developed or overpowered the other. Until they learn language, children absorb experience using a kind of nonverbal "thinking," characterized later in the brain's development as a right hemispheric function. When language begins, each hemisphere seems to be equally developed. In its structural and biochemical sense, the brain doesn't reach its full maturation until about age 12.

By maturation, the left hemisphere typically develops as the dominant side, controlling the verbal and logical functions of the brain, while the right hemisphere controls spatial and visual functions. For many years, such development was thought to be genetically predetermined and unaffected by life experiences. Today, however, this belief has changed. Although the acquisition of language appears to be universal, we now recognize that the abilities required for expression and reasoning are not automatic. Watching television threatens the development of these abilities because it requires a suspension of active cognition.

Limit Viewing to Stimulate Imaginations

The American Academy of Pediatrics recommends that children under the age of two not watch TV or videos, and that older children watch only one to two hours per day of nonviolent, educational TV. Young children watching TV are routinely described as transfixed, passive, and nonverbal. One of television's appeals for parents is that it serves as an immediate way to silence and sedate active toddlers. But such nonverbal absorption does more than simply relax and amuse preschoolers. Language spoken by actors on TV does not have the same effect as real-life language experiences. The Journal of Broadcasting reported that language skills among American children declined as TV viewing time increased.

In real life, conversation is reciprocal and participatory; it allows time for reflection, questions, and encouragement. Television, how-

Aspects of TV that Have Gotten Worse

	1993	2005
Too much sex	33%	22%
Too much violence	38%	21%
Dislike reality TV	---	17%
Immorality, bad values	9%	16%
Pointless/No plots/No substance	10%	13%
Bad influence on children	12%	11%
Language/Swearing	8%	10%
Just don't like shows now	8%	7%
Bad for families	4%	6%
Favorite show is no longer on	4%	5%
Just going for ratings	2%	5%
Don't like sitcoms/Not funny	4%	1%
Dislike real-life crime programs	1%	1%
Other	4%	6%
Don't know	2%	1%

Taken from: Pew Research Center, "TV Choices Okay But Content Has Gotten Worse," April 17, 2005

ever, is a one-way street, and you had better stay glued, ask no questions, and take no time for thought, because the next scene will appear in seconds and there is no rewind. As a result, children learn not to think but to remain passive and unresponsive to whatever stimulus appears before them. Television conditions them to absorb images without mental effort and to expect rapid change. Since young children's questions and imaginations are the cornerstone of their learning processes, remaining unresponsive hour after hour, day after day, year after year surely affects their intellectual, emotional, and moral development. Fantasy play, a critical component of childhood, allows children to explore different situations with varying responses and outcomes. While books and storytelling nourish fantasy play, fantasy watching does not foster the same reaction. The US Department of Education reported that 81 percent of children ages two to seven watch TV unsupervised, which means that young children enter a world of fantasy without the guidance and oversight of an adult. Research by the Yale University Family Television and Consultation Center reveals that imagination decreases as TV watching increases. TV teaches children to be amused by its images instead of encouraging kids to create their own. It dulls the mind by the power of its fast-moving pictures, supplanting the mental activity necessary to follow in the mind's eye a book or a storyteller's tale. The Yale Center reports that complex language and grammar skills are directly linked to fantasy play, and that children who create fantasy play are more tolerant, peaceful, patient, and happy.

The Backlash of TV's Positive Effects

Many children become habituated to TV by their parents, who desire a break from their child's activity and attention. However, the short-term benefit of a quiet, mesmerized child may actually lead to a greater dependence on adult supervision by creating children who are less capable of amusing themselves. By supplanting their imaginations, creating fast-paced pictures, and transforming active minds into passive recipients, TV teaches mental lethargy.

For a child raised on hourly doses of TV, boredom is a common component of later childhood. In refusing to use TV during the preschool years, parents may save themselves from constantly having to create amusements for their children.

The best way to keep TV from becoming an issue with children, of course, is not to begin using it. If a TV is present in the home, it is vital to establish clear rules on its use and to maintain these rules. Never make TV a reward or a punishment; this only heightens its power. When starting the withdrawal from TV, explain why you are making these changes and that it is not a punishment. The first month will be the most difficult. Children may cry or plead, but you can remain firm if you keep in mind that you are freeing them from an addiction.

Do Something Else

It is also imperative that you help your children learn how to fill the time that they formerly spent watching TV. Work with them to nurture interests, discover hobbies, and explore new possibilities. Begin a nightly read-aloud for the entire family. Take walks after breakfast or dinner. Share your hobbies—sewing, knitting, baking bread—with them. Learn to play instruments and make music as a family. Encourage children to help with work around the house and yard. Visit neighbors and relatives. Tell stories and pass on your family history. Build a birdhouse. Go bowling. Go sledding. Finger paint. Color. Practice yoga together. Involve your children in the daily activities of the house, and encourage yourself and your family to rekindle the flame of exploration and discovery, away from the draw of the flickering blue screen.

EVALUATING THE AUTHOR'S ARGUMENTS:

Ann Vorisek White argues that television is unhealthy, especially for children. Think back on your own experiences watching television, both recently and earlier in your childhood. How do you feel about television? Do you think that your television watching has been unhealthy or not? What would you do if there were no television?

Television Is Not Always Harmful

Anna Quindlen

In the following viewpoint, author and social commentator Anna Quindlen makes the argument that far from being always harmful, television actually serves an important social purpose. Television, Quindlen notes, shows the lives of ordinary people, such as those affected by Hurricane Katrina. Politicians and others in power should utilize this important medium to reconnect with the world outside of Washington, Quindlen argues, and realize that they themselves can also be filmed and broadcast to the nation. Anna Quindlen writes a regular column for *Newsweek*, in addition to writing novels, of which she has published four.

"You're not qualified to govern this country . . . if you don't understand the uses of TV. . . . Those in public life should be required to watch it."

AS YOU READ, CONSIDER THE FOLLOWING QUESTIONS:
1. What is one result cited by the author of the president being divorced from the normal human experience?
2. What does Quindlen suggest the president do to "transcend his isolation"?
3. What percentage of Americans watch TV news for more than an hour, according to the author?

On the second day of judge John Roberts's confirmation hearings, CNN's Jeff Greenfield felt moved to ask a question. The guest was Sen. Charles Grassley of Iowa, and Greenfield inquired why his fellows on the Judiciary Committee felt the need to use their limited time for bloviation instead of actually asking the judge questions. Senator Grassley replied in one word: "television."

I can reply to that in three words: aw, come on.

Members of Congress have had more than a quarter century to get used to the idea that cameras are recording their proceedings, and that this is an invaluable thing for the American people. Watching the hearings to decide whether Roberts should become chief justice was quite illuminating from several collateral perspectives. How could senators complain that

they had not learned enough about the nominee when so many of them had wasted their allotted time giving pocket stump speeches? How come the aides who sit behind them don't realize that they, too, will be on camera, and that therefore they should not behave like small children in church? And didn't Sen. Tom Coburn think anyone in the room would notice that he was doing a crossword puzzle? Isn't it strange how these people are both mesmerized by the cameras and weirdly insensible to them?

You're not qualified to govern this country at this moment in time if you don't understand the uses of TV. In fact, those in public life should be required to watch it. It's like Google Earth for the national psyche, hovering over the landscape, zooming in. Much of what it zooms in on makes you wonder what we've come to. Are teenage girls and their parents really as venal, acquisitive and without standards as "My Super Sweet 16" would suggest? Has the revolution in science and technology in our time really led inexorably to the breast implants (and man tans) of "Dr. 90210"?

But saying that there's a lot of junk on TV and that's why you won't watch (or, for purists, won't have a set in the house) is like saying you won't read books because there are a fair amount of cheesy ones published. Just look at the government debacle surrounding Hurricane Katrina. Apparently they didn't know. This is mind-boggling to those of us who understand how to work a remote. Every network, every moment, was showing what looked like a disaster movie with the most terrifying special effects possible. And everywhere there were the same sentiments, hand-lettered on placards, painted on roofs, screamed by women with children outside the Superdome: help.

We Americans were ahead of the administration curve because apparently its members weren't watching TV. Lots of huff-and-puffs in D.C. don't. Some of them make the argument that they're too busy to channel-surf. Bull. The members of Congress find time in their schedules to consume finger food with lobbyists. The president currently holds the world record for vacationing by a head of state.

The nature of his job is that he's divorced from normal human experience. He doesn't have to buy a gallon of milk or a gallon of gas.

More People Watching TV Than Ever

Minutes Tuned in to Television per 24-Hour Period

Television Year (Sept.–Sept.)	Homes Avg. Hours: Minutes per Day	Persons 2+ Avg. Hours: Minutes per Day
2005–2006	8:14	4:35
2004–2005	8:11	4:32
2003–2004	8:01	4:25
2002–2003	7:55	4:25
2001–2002	7:42	4:18
2000–2001	7:39	4:15
1999–2000	7:31	4:06
1998–1999	7:24	4:00
1997–1998	7:15	3:58
1996–1997	7:12	3:56
1995–1996	7:15	3:59

Taken from: Nielsen Media Research, "Nielsen Media Research Reports Television's Popularity is Still Growing," September 21, 2006

It has been suggested that by watching television, politicians can learn more about and stay connected to the people they serve.

He doesn't hear people talking about his shortcomings or their own despair. Everything seems to take him by surprise, so that while we were watching the end of the world in New Orleans he was giving some lame speech spelling out how many pounds of ice were being sent south. If he'd been watching all those black women with hungry babies on their hips in New Orleans, he would have known that we were heading into the teeth of a national storm on poverty and race as devastating as any hurricane.

But the president doesn't see what we see. He doesn't know what we know. He needs to find some way to transcend his isolation, and one way is to watch TV. Instead of those stagy red-white-blue events with the cheering crowds, he might want to take a look at some episodes of "Cops" to see what's really going on in parts of the nation. Maybe the sight of the battered buildings of Fallujah, once stores and schools and homes, would provide a clue to why some Iraqis aren't thrilled to have us there. As a lifelong print person, I have to admit sadly that the small screen owns some of the biggest stories of our time, because of the footage, because of the immediacy, because of the range. More than 30 percent of us watch TV news for more than an hour. The average home has three TV sets.

A certain snobbery has developed around the notion of TV viewing, a certain "let them watch 'Raymond'" attitude that television is déclassé, a thing best left to the masses. Well, it's the masses who decide elections, and who live with their results as well. Think of it this way: The Founding Fathers are sitting around in Philadelphia and New York, the 13 Colonies stretching up the coast and down, Virginia and Rhode Island a long slog on horseback. And suddenly someone offers them a way to know what people are thinking, on farms, in towns, from the North to the South. Not a perfect way, not a way that tells you everything you need to know, but a way nonetheless.

They'd jump at the chance. So should their successors.

EVALUATING THE AUTHOR'S ARGUMENTS:

Anna Quindlen, author of the viewpoint you just read, believes that television helps society by providing a view of ordinary life. The author of the preceding viewpoint, Ann Vorisek White, takes a negative view of television, arguing that it is damaging to people's creative minds. After reading both viewpoints, which argument do you find more compelling? Support your answer with evidence from the viewpoints.

Viewpoint

3

Television Contributes to Childhood Obesity

Steven Gortmaker

"Television watching is directly linked with obesity."

Steven Gortmaker is a professor at the Harvard School of Public Health. In the following viewpoint, he argues that television has directly contributed to increased rates of childhood obesity. Two factors contribute to this trend, Gortmaker writes: the sedentary lifestyle of sitting in front of the TV and exposure to commercials advertising unhealthy fast food, junk food, and soda. Parents should limit their children's exposure to TV in general, Gortmaker argues, as well as their exposure to commercials. Television should be considered a treat, rather than a regular occurrence, in Gortmaker's opinion.

AS YOU READ, CONSIDER THE FOLLOWING QUESTIONS:
1. For how long has the connection between television watching and obesity been established, according to Gortmaker?
2. Of what foods are kids consuming too much and too little, according to the author?
3. What two steps does Gortmaker suggest parents take to ensure their kids live a healthier lifestyle?

Steven Gortmaker, "Twin Scourges for Kids: Obesity and Television," *Boston Globe,* October 19, 2004, p. A23. Reproduced by permission of the author.

Our children are spending more time than ever in front of the television. Their viewing opportunities are no longer contained to afternoons and Saturday mornings; many networks are devoted to entertaining them all day. While parents may be cognizant of the negative effects that excessive sedentary behavior can have on children, we may not be as aware of the persistent messages children receive from advertisers about unhealthy foods. The food industry spends billions of dollars each year to woo our children to their high calorie products that possess little or no nutritional value. On average a child watching TV sees a commercial from the food industry every five minutes.

Childhood obesity is a rapidly spreading epidemic in the United States. Since 1980, the proportion of overweight children ages 6 to 11 has more than doubled, and the rate for overweight adolescents has tripled. The connection between television viewing and obesity was established almost two decades ago, yet our habits have not changed to protect our children.

A study in Boston revealed that 60 percent of middle school age children have a television in their bedroom, and a national study showed that 75 percent of parents do not care how much television their children watch.

Kids Are Exposed to Junk Food Ads

Television watching is directly linked with obesity. The excessive sedentary time in front of the television is, coupled with, and compounded by, intense exposure to advertisements promoting so called "junk foods"—low nutritional quality, high calorie foods such as sugar sweetened beverages. Exposure to food advertisements has been linked to an overall increase in calorie intake, overconsumption of fast food, candy, and soda, as well as underconsumption of fruits and vegetables. Kids are being taught to lead unhealthy lives from a very young age, and we are seeing the effects of the bad habits

FAST FACT

The percentage of American children who are obese has risen from seven percent in 1976-1980 to fifteen percent in 2006, according to the Healthy People Library Project.

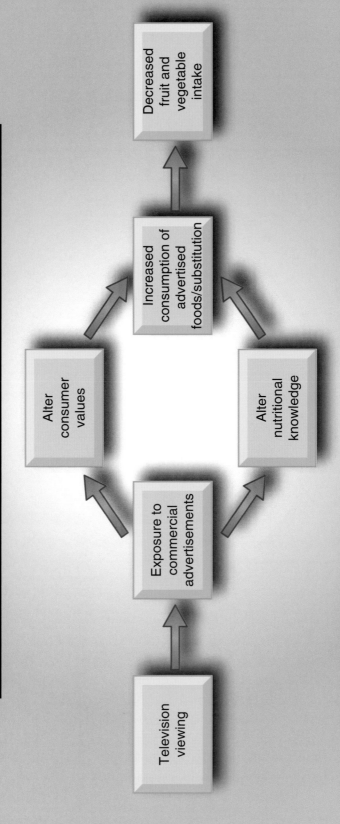

TV Viewing Patterns Influence Fruit and Vegetable Consumption in Children by Encouraging Consumption of Advertised Foods

Television viewing

Exposure to commercial advertisements

Alter consumer values

Alter nutritional knowledge

Increased consumption of advertised foods/substitution

Decreased fruit and vegetable intake

Taken from: Karen E. Peterson, "Television Viewing in Obesity Prevention & control in Youth," Harvard School of Public Health, 2003

Texas is using television commercials of their own to help combat childhood obesity, which some believe is exacerbated by ads for junk food.

We are not suggesting throwing out your television or even prohibiting it. Limit your child's viewing time to less than two hours a day and make "junk food" a treat rather than a staple in their diet. Children learn their health lifestyle from their parents and other significant adults in their lives. We must serve as role models and help them to make healthy decisions and cultivate good habits by restricting television, encouraging more active pursuits and educating our children about healthy eating habits. In the battle against obesity we need to lead with our actions as well as our words.

EVALUATING THE AUTHOR'S ARGUMENTS:

Steven Gortmaker and Douglas J. Wood, author of the following viewpoint, disagree on the link between childhood obesity and television, but they agree that parents should be responsible for limiting children's television watching. Other critics, however, believe that food advertisers should be prohibited from marketing to children. In your opinion, who should take responsibility for the commercials children see on television, parents or advertisers? Explain your answer, citing from the viewpoints.

Television Ads Are Not Necessarily Responsible for Obesity

Douglas J. Wood

"*Do we isolate young children from marketing, and then expect them to become savvy consumers the moment they are . . . exposed to commercial content?*"

Douglas J. Wood is an advertising executive with the firm Reed Smith. He is also the author of the book *Please Be Ad-vised: The Legal Guide for the Advertising Executive*. In the following viewpoint, Wood argues that punishing the advertising industry for childhood obesity is neither fair nor effective. Parents should take responsibility for what their children see on television commercials and teach them to be savvy consumers, Wood maintains, rather than prohibiting advertisers from successfully marketing their products. Moreover, advertisers should not have their right to free speech restricted because parents are not teaching their children proper nutritional habits, he argues.

The foes of advertising to children have been very vocal in recent months and are getting the ear of numerous policymakers—despite espousing some deeply flawed logic.

Holding children's welfare as a golden cane with which to flog the advertising industry, they seek to place the blame for child obesity and other social concerns in the lap of business. They flaunt statistics about the number of hours children watch television, and the expansion of advertising into schools and homes via computer. They ignore statistics that show the highest correlation to childhood obesity is parental

Some believe that it is the parent's responsibility to help their children learn how to make decisions about the commercials they see on television.

obesity. From these figures and anecdotes, child ad crusaders leap to the unsubstantiated and troubling conclusion that all ads allegedly targeted to the very young should be killed.

Regulation by the FTC Recommended

In a February 2004 report, the American Psychological Association [APA] linked children's misperceptions about proper nutritional habits to television viewing, and blamed ads for the development of positive attitudes toward tobacco and alcohol. Concluding that young children have a limited ability to recognize and defend against commercial persuasion, the APA believes advertising "directed to . . . children below the age of roughly 7-8 years should be considered unfair." The APA suggests a return of jurisdiction to the Federal Trade Commission [FTC] to regulate children's advertising under the unfairness standard—the standard under which the FTC tried to ban children's advertising in the late '70s, before being pulled back by Congress.

In the same week [of February 2004], the Henry J. Kaiser Family Foundation issued a report concluding that food advertising is a significant contributor to obesity in children. The Kaiser study suggests policy considerations such as banning children's food advertising altogether, or prohibiting product placement. Congressional hearings to address the issue have been scheduled. . . . Senator Joseph Lieberman called for a FTC investigation into the practices of companies marketing unhealthy foods to children.

Ads for Children Are Not Necessarily Harmful

Add to the debate a recent court ruling. In *Mainstream vs. FTC,* a case involving a challenge to the national do-not-call registry, the U.S. 10th Circuit Court of Appeals found that restricting commercial speech on the basis of anecdotal evidence was an appropriate legislative initiative. The APA study will likely be seen as being more than just anecdotal evidence.

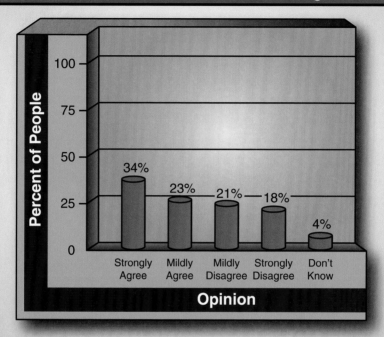

Percent of People Who Agreed or Disagreed That Government Should Restrict Commercials that Target Children

Taken from: First Amendment Center, "State of the First Amendment," 2005

In all this hysteria there's some good news for marketers in that studies show children's purchase requests are influenced by ads, characters and celebrities used to sell products and in-store promotions—their work works. Of course the child-ad foes would punish this success.

Never mind the obvious solution—that parents, as household decision makers, are capable of monitoring the amount and types of TV programming their children watch, which products are purchased, how often fast food should be consumed, and whether their tot stands to benefit from the latest toy trend.

Never mind that no evidence has been presented that children over the age of 8 represent a generation of automatons conditioned by years of unfair advertising during their formative years. Ask any teenager today what he or she thinks of advertising and you'll hear a skeptical response and a consumer entirely attuned to the purposes behind these messages. Whatever the harm done during those first eight years the APA seems so concerned about, it does not appear to be lasting. Perhaps that's because there wasn't any harm.

Never mind the possibility that parents may appreciate that their children have greater programming choices—options that would shrink fast if the advertising that supports them were to go away.

The APA acknowledges that banning ads to 8-and-unders would limit marketers to focusing on older children, but blithely points to other countries that have taken this approach, including Australia, Canada, the U.K. and Sweden. Never mind that the statistics in Quebec and Sweden show that bans had no effect on the problems sought to be corrected.

Advertisers Must Defend Their Rights

As importantly, do we isolate young children from marketing, and then expect them to become savvy consumers the moment they are deemed mature enough to be exposed to commercial content?

Whether it's candy or fries, there's no doubt too much of a good thing can lead to harm. But limiting free speech won't guarantee a reduction in overindulgence. It will ensure more limited competition, fewer consumer options, and, invariably, inferior goods and services.

Clearly, the solution is self-regulation, provided it works. And there's every reason to believe it does. The Children's Advertising Review Unit [CARU] of the Council of Better Business Bureaus adjudicated more than 140 cases [in 2003], convincing advertisers to modify content more than 130 times. When one decided to ignore CARU, the FTC fined the advertiser $400,000. Working in tandem, self-regulation with regulatory muscle works.

Advertisers should not run from their success, nor should they cede ground to those who would punish them for being effective. Advertisers must diligently defend their right to communicate with American families through the universe of media options the industry helps finance. And they should trust parents to draw sensible lines for their kids.

EVALUATING THE AUTHOR'S ARGUMENTS:

Author Douglas J. Wood is opposed to the idea of banning television ads for unhealthy foods. However, he does not dispute that the advertising industry markets directly to children. In your opinion, is it ethical or unethical to aim junk food commercials at children? Should these marketers be permitted to do this, or should they be stopped? Explain your answers.

Chapter 2

What Is Society's Relationship to Television?

Television is an ever-present force in the world today.

Television Content Should Be Censored

Tony Perkins

"Broadcasters [may] . . . use a spectrum of the public airwaves as long as they abide by the public interest obligation . . . enforced by the FCC."

Tony Perkins is the president of the conservative family-values organization, the Family Research Council. In this viewpoint, he argues that the Federal Communications Commission (FCC) has a duty to regulate and control material on television as well as in other media. In 2006, the FCC proposed an increase in the fines it could levy on violators of "decency" regulations in order to have more power. This is an excellent move, Perkins argues. Children should not be exposed to strong language or sexuality on television, and it is the government's job to protect them by censoring this sort of material, he contends.

AS YOU READ, CONSIDER THE FOLLOWING QUESTIONS:
1. What is the FCC's definition of indecent material, as quoted by Perkins?
2. Define the word *"disingenuous"* within the context of the viewpoint.
3. What do the sitting FCC commissioners want to do to further control indecency on the airwaves, according to Perkins?

Overcoming powerful opposition . . . , Congress has provided American families greater protection from indecent broadcasting. Late [in December 2006] Jack Valenti, lobbyist extraordinaire for Hollywood and all it stands for, told an audience, "No one today knows what is indecent." Since then I've been trying to find Mr. Valenti's address so I could send him the most recent edition of the Merriam-Webster dictionary—which defines indecent as being "grossly unseemly or offensive to manners or morals."

If that is not enough for Hollywood's mouthpiece I also have a copy of the Federal Communications Commission's (FCC's) regulations which state: "Material is indecent if, in context, it depicts or describes sexual or excretory organs or activities in terms patently offensive as measured by contemporary community standards for the broadcast medium."

It might be news to Jack and his cohorts that since 1978 the Supreme Court has recognized that broadcast licenses are, in essence, a contract

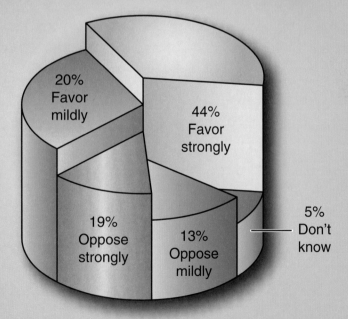

Percent of Americans Who Favor or Oppose an Increase in Broadcast Indecency Fines

20% Favor mildly

44% Favor strongly

19% Oppose strongly

13% Oppose mildly

5% Don't know

Taken from: First Amendment Center, "State of the First Amendment," 2005

between the government and those wishing to utilize airwaves owned by the American public. Broadcasters are granted the freedom to use a spectrum of the public airwaves as long as they abide by the public interest obligation set forth by Congress and enforced by the FCC.

Broadcasting Industry Is Indecent

Now it is no surprise that Jack doesn't know decency, since the industry he defends has been defining decency down over the last few decades. The occasion that he used to make his statement was at the National Association of Broadcasters annual convention where he was introducing (and

this is no joke) a $300 million advertising blitz to help parents control the shows their children watch. While, as a parent myself, I believe parents need to play an important role in what their children watch, I also realize for many parents it is impossible to regulate 24 hours a day what their children see or don't see.

This attempt by broadcasters is a disingenuous way to counter efforts in Congress to increase the amount of the fines at least tenfold that the FCC can levy (currently the fines are a mere $32,500). I call the attempt disingenuous because around the same time as Jack's speech, CBS and other broadcast networks asked a U.S. appeals court to overturn FCC decisions that found broadcasters violated decency standards. The FCC had proposed $3.6 million in fines against the networks for decency violations, including about $3.3 million against CBS stations for airing an episode of the murder mystery show *Without a Trace* that depicted teenagers engaged in an "orgy." CBS's first response to the fines was to rebroadcast the offending episode.

Before you feel bad for poor CBS keep in mind that just the estimated ad revenue for 12 episodes of *Without a Trace* is over $32 million—a $3 million fine is just considered the cost of doing business. The true mystery in the scenario is why Senate Commerce Chairman Ted Stevens (R-AK) supports the networks' plan but has fought behind the scenes to murder the legislation that would raise the FCC fines.

Reverend Al Sharpton talks with the media after meeting with the FCC to discuss stricter regulations on airplay for music artists who promote violence.

FCC Should Work to End Indecency

I'll be honest, I don't watch much television. The last program I can recall watching on broadcast television was *ALF,* a sitcom about a furry alien who crash-landed on Earth. Yet when I sat down and watched some of the shows that the FCC has recently fined I was the one who felt like an alien from another planet. The scenes, depicting under-age sex, intense sexual situations and utterances (I won't repeat them in case my parents read this), clearly fit within the Supreme Court's definition of indecency. Traditionally the FCC has sat idly by while broadcast television tried to redefine our culture—I have been assured that will no longer be the case.

We now have an FCC that is concerned about what children are exposed to through the public airwaves. All the sitting FCC Commissioners have voiced support for an increase in indecency fines and FCC Chairman Kevin Martin has already increased the number of fines levied against those who would abuse the public airwaves.

However, unless these fines are increased these multi-billion dollar broadcasters will never get the message. Broadcasters need to clean up or pay up. For too long Hollywood has held the "controls" in the effort to define our culture. Thanks to Congress's action, concerned parents may now begin to take it back.

EVALUATING THE AUTHOR'S ARGUMENTS:

In the viewpoint you just read, author Tony Perkins cites the FCC's definition of indecent material: "Material is indecent if, in context, it depicts or describes sexual or excretory organs or activities in terms patently offensive as measured by contemporary community standards for the broadcast medium." Do you agree that material gauged by this definition should be available on television? Can you think of situations in which this sort of material would be educational? Explain your answer using an example from your own experiences.

Television Content Should Not Be Censored

Jacob Sullum

> "TV is not a criminal invading our homes; it's an invited guest. If we think he might misbehave, it's up to us to keep an eye on him."

In the following viewpoint, Jacob Sullum presents the argument that the government should not be in charge of regulating the television airwaves. The Federal Communications Commission's (FCC) efforts to control indecent scenes on television apply only to broadcast TV anyway, Sullum points out, while many Americans watch satellite and cable television, which are not subject to regulation. The FCC wants to extend its regulations to cable and satellite, which begins to impinge on free speech. Since new technology enables parents to block unsuitable material, Sullum argues that censorship should be a personal decision, not a governmental one. Jacob Sullum is a senior editor of *Reason* magazine.

Jacob Sullum, "Indecent Proposal," *Reason*, June 7, 2006. Copyright 2006 by Reason Foundation, 3415 S. Sepulveda Blvd., Suite 400, Los Angeles, CA 90034, www.reason.com. Reproduced by permission.

The overwhelming support on Capitol Hill for legislation that will dramatically increase the fines for broadcasting "indecent" programming suggests there's broad agreement that the federal government should get serious about cleaning up TV. But the more closely you examine the justifications for this crackdown, the clearer it becomes that the ban on broadcast indecency either goes too far or does not go far enough.

Fear of FCC fines led the public television broadcaster to warn stations against airing an uncensored documentary about these U.S. Army soldiers in Iraq.

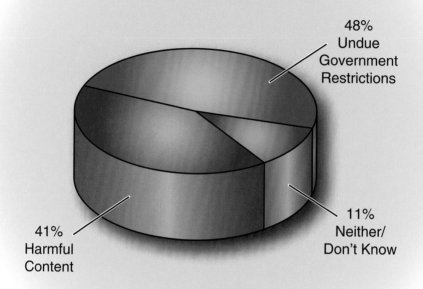

Which is Greater Danger: Harmful Content or Government Censorship?

48%
Undue
Government
Restrictions

41%
Harmful
Content

11%
Neither/
Don't Know

Taken from: Pew Research Center, "Support for Tougher Indecency Measures, But Worries About Government Instrusiveness," April 15, 2005

Sen. Sam Brownback (R-Kan.), who introduced the Senate version of the bill raising the maximum penalty for broadcast indecency from $32,500 to $325,000 per violation, says businesses that use "the nation's public airwaves" have special obligations. "Broadcast spectrum is a very valuable and scarce national resource," he says. "In return for a license, each broadcaster must not air indecent content between the hours of 6 a.m. [and] 10 p.m."

Broadcast spectrum is a "national resource" only because the government insisted on nationalizing it. There's no reason in principle why the right to transmit at a certain frequency in a certain area could not be treated the same way as the right to graze cattle or build a sky-scraper on a particular piece of land. Broadcast licenses already are de facto property, bought and sold along with stations, except that the Federal Communications Commission [FCC] occasionally clobbers broadcasters with fines if it does not like what they air.

A Violation of Rights

Nor is it clear why using a pub-lic resource to send a message should affect the speaker's First Amendment rights, making him subject to government content regulation. Newspapers are deliv-ered via "the public roads," and Web site information travels on

FAST FACT

The Federal Communi-cations Commission was created by Congress in 1934.

wires across public property (sometimes even through "the public airwaves"), but that doesn't mean forcing journalists and bloggers to be "decent" is constitutionally permissible.

In any case, for the politicians and activists who want to protect children from the shows their parents let them watch, the "public airwaves" argument does not go far enough. Nearly nine out of 10 American households get TV via cable or satellite, modes of transmis-sion that are not subject to indecency rules.

As Senate Commerce Committee Chairman Ted Stevens (R-Alaska) has pointed out, that distinction makes little sense. "Most viewers don't differentiate between over the air and cable," he told the National Association of Broadcasters last year, and "cable is a greater violator in the indecency arena."

Censor All or None

It was music to the ears of broadcasters losing viewers to the racier shows on cable. House Commerce Committee Chairman Joe Barton (R-Texas) agreed that "it's not fair to subject over-the-air broadcasters to one set of rules and subject cable and satellite to no rules." Barton said he would join Stevens in supporting the extension of content restrictions to cable and satellite "if we can work out the constitutional questions."

That part may be tricky. The Supreme Court has applied "strict scrutiny" to content regulation of cable TV, finding a "key difference between cable television and the broadcasting media" in "the capacity to block unwanted channels on a household-by-household basis."

Censor from the Home

Yet in the age of the V-chip and content ratings, parents (even the small minority without cable or satellite TV) have the ability to block not just entire channels but particular kinds of programming, including violence and other potentially objectionable content that goes far beyond the sexual and excretory stuff covered by the FCC's indecency rules. Instead of banning "Deadwood" and "The Sopranos," or banishing them to the FCC's late-night "safe harbor," how about asking parents to take some responsibility for monitoring what their kids watch?

When it upheld the FCC's content rules back in 1978, the Supreme Court said "indecent material presented over the airwaves confronts the citizen... in the privacy of the home," as if TV were a robber or a rapist. But TV is not a criminal invading our homes; it's an invited guest. If we think he might misbehave, it's up to us to keep an eye on him.

EVALUATING THE AUTHOR'S ARGUMENTS:

Jacob Sullum believes that the government should not be responsible for censoring television, whereas the previous viewpoint argues the opposite. Which viewpoint would you support? Which arguments would you highlight as most important to uphold your claim?

Television Leads to Moral Decline

Brian Fitzpatrick

> "The more a person watches television, the less likely he will be to accept responsibility for his own life and for his obligations to the people around him."

Brian Fitzpatrick is the senior editor for the Culture and Media Institute (CMI) and the author of the Institute's special report, *The Media Assault on American Values*.

In this viewpoint, he argues that television viewing is responsible for significant degradation of morals and character. The media, Fitzpatrick says, undermine Americans' fundamental values. The aforementioned report was supported by an extensive survey, which found that heavy television viewers, those who watch more than four hours per evening, are less likely than light viewers, those who watch one hour or less per evening, to value honesty, charity, religion, and responsibility, among other things. Fitzpatrick explains that the American people recognize the fall of morality, and many people believe that television is responsible.

AS YOU READ, CONSIDER THE FOLLOWING QUESTIONS:
1. According to the author, does the survey explore a cause-and-effect relationship between exposure to the media and behavior?

Brian Fitzpatrick, "Does Watching TV Damage Character?" www.humanevents.com, June 13, 2007. Reproduced by permission.

2. What percentage of heavy television viewers state that homosexuality is wrong?
3. Which values do the media undermine, according to
Fitzpatrick?

Couch potatoes, beware—someday you might be saying "the
TV made me do it."
        A new [2007] special report by the Culture and Media
Institute (CMI) indicates that watching too much television could be
hazardous to your moral health.

The report, *The Media Assault on American Values*, reveals that media
messages appear to be undermining the pillars of America's cultural
edifice: strength of character, sexual morality and respect for God. The
report is based on findings of a major scientific survey commissioned
by CMI, a division of the Media Research Center.

More TV Means Permissive Morals

The National Cultural Values Survey reveals a striking correlation
between greater exposure to television and permissive moral views.
Heavy television viewers (four hours or more per evening) are less
committed to character virtues like honesty and charity, and more
permissive about sex, abortion and homosexuality. Light television
viewers (one hour or less per evening) are more likely to attend religious services and live their lives by God's principles.

The survey wasn't designed to identify causal relationships between
media and behavior, but it did collect information about television
viewing habits. The results are compelling.

Let's look at the foundation of good character—personal responsibility. According to the survey, the more a person watches television,
the less likely he will be to accept responsibility for his own life and
for his obligations to the people around him.

More TV Means Less Responsibility

Personal responsibility begins with providing for your own needs, but
the news media and movie directors like Michael Moore consistently
preach that people should look to government, not rely on themselves.
Heavy television viewers are much likelier than light viewers to expect

government to provide retirement (64 percent to 43 percent) and health care (63 percent to 48 percent).

Another aspect of personal responsibility is taking care of your neighbor's needs. The media's voyeuristic, celebrity-driven entertainment and "news" programming promotes narcissism, not charity. Not surprisingly, light viewers are more likely than heavy viewers to contribute time or treasure to every kind of cause. Heavy viewers are more than twice as likely not to give at all (24 percent to 11 percent), and not to volunteer (56 percent to 27 percent).

The Media Undermine Religious Values

The pattern persists with sexual morality. Is sex outside of marriage, the way Hollywood incessantly depicts it, always wrong? 39 percent of light viewers say so. Only 26 percent of heavy viewers agree. 55 percent of light viewers say homosexuality, another Hollywood hobbyhorse, is wrong, but only 43 percent of heavy viewers.

The media's continual portrayal of clergy and believers as moral reprobates, and outrages like showing God in bed with a woman (both Fox's *Family Guy* and Comedy Central's *Sarah Silverman Program*), appear to be eroding the nation's devotion to religion. 32 percent of heavy viewers say they live by God's values above their own, significantly less than the 43 percent of light viewers.

> **FAST FACT**
>
> According to a 2007 survey for the Culture and Media Institute, 73 percent of those polled think American entertainment media have a negative effect on the nation's commitment to moral values.

Overall, 74 percent of Americans say our moral values are weaker than they were 20 years ago, and 48 percent say values are much weaker. That's another way of saying they see eroding character, lower sexual standards, and diminished respect for God—precisely the values the media undermine.

The Media Is Responsible

In consequence, overwhelming majorities hold the media responsible for contributing to moral decline.

Television programs like Survivor: Cook Islands have been criticized for pitting people of different races against each other.

Ten Americans believe Hollywood is harming the nation's moral condition for every one who thinks Hollywood is helping. The numbers? 73 percent to 7 percent. For the news media, the ratio is five to one: 54 percent harming the nation's moral standards, and just 11 percent helping.

The bottom line: Most Americans believe the nation's morality is slipping. These people name the media as the second greatest factor in the moral decline, exceeded only by the family.

EVALUATING THE AUTHOR'S ARGUMENTS:

The author of this viewpoint argues that television watching lends itself heavily to moral decay. What might Fitzpatrick's suggestions be for slowing or correcting this decline? Do you think he would push for government intervention and censorship, or encourage change on a local or individual level?

Television Does Not Lead to Moral Decline

Ronald Bailey

"Watching TV... does have some bad aspects— one can always get too much of a good thing—but it is hardly the instrument of mental, cultural, and moral degradation it is so often portrayed as."

In this viewpoint, Ronald Bailey argues that television is not significantly responsible for "mental, cultural, and moral degradation." Bailey recognizes the harm that excessive viewing can cause, but he argues that it is an individual's responsibility to avoid that obvious harm. Bailey uses a personal example to demonstrate how television can be inspiring for one's moral and personal success. Even considering the huge number of TVs now filling American households, he contends that television viewing cannot be the factor most to blame for obesity, violence, and teen sexual activity. In the end, Bailey presents television as an activity, much like any other, to fill up free time. Ronald Bailey is an award-winning science correspondent for *Reason*, a libertarian magazine.

AS YOU READ, CONSIDER THE FOLLOWING QUESTIONS:
1. According to Ronald Bailey, why did a man sue his cable company?

Ronald Bailey, "We All Know That TV Is Bad for Us," www.reason.com, December 29, 2004. Copyright 2004 by Reason Foundation, 3415 S. Sepulveda Blvd., Suite 400, Los Angeles, CA 90034, www.reason.com. Reproduced by permission.

2. What does Bailey name as the percentage of Americans owning television sets in 1961, up from nine percent in 1950?
3. How does the author challenge the claims of the "bill of indictment on television?"

Watching TV is a lot like smoking. People know all the crummy side-effects and continue to do it anyway," declares one typical anti-TV rant. "Most smokers are aware that their habit can cause cancer and emphysema. Most TV watchers know that their habit is mind-numbing and wasteful."

A man recently threatened to sue his cable company. Why? "I believe that the reason I smoke and drink every day and my wife is overweight is because we watched TV every day for the last four years," he claimed. These assertions regarding the ill effects of TV seem so obviously true that few even question them. Surely reams of academic studies over the decades have amply confirmed television's pernicious mental and moral influences.

Or have they? Is the conventional anti-TV wisdom true?

Television Can Inspire

When I was a boy growing up on a dairy farm in southwest Virginia in the early 1960s, the black-and-white television that dominated our living room was a magic kaleidoscopic window onto a wider and more alluring world. It enlarged my sense of what was possible. It showed me different ways of life that didn't involve chasing after brute stupid Holsteins twice a day. As silly as the old programs might seem, one could be inspired by images of Danny Thomas living in a high-rise apartment in Manhattan or the dolphin Flipper rescuing people in the Gulf of Mexico. Television wasn't the only thing that motivated me to flee the farm up the nearly completed Interstate 81, but it helped.

However, our self-appointed moral guardians and cultural mandarins have largely been blind to the liberating aspects of television. Then Federal Communications Commission chairman Newton Minow famously declared on May 9, 1961, that television was a "vast wasteland." He invited his listeners to sit through a full day's pro-

Bill Cosby addresses a conference intended to promote the creation of television programs for young people that foster diversity.

gramming, promising: "You will see a procession of game shows, violence, audience-participation shows, formula comedies about totally unbelievable families, blood and thunder, mayhem, violence, sadism, murder, western bad men, western good men, private eyes, gangsters, more violence and cartoons. And, endlessly, commercials—many screaming, cajoling and offending. And most of all, boredom."

Curmudgeonly cultural critic Neil Postman piled on in his 1986 book *Amusing Ourselves to Death: Public Discourse in the Age of Show Business*, claiming that "a great media-metaphor shift (from typography to television) has taken place in America, with the result that the content of much of our public discourse has become dangerous nonsense."

TVs In Homes

Despite the hectoring from bureaucrats and intellectuals, the nation continued to tune in. In 1950 only nine percent of American households owned a television set. By 1961, when Minow pronounced his execrations on the boob tube, nearly 90 percent of U.S. living rooms were bathed in blue light each night. By 2001, according to the Census Bureau, 98.2 percent of American households owned at least one of the 248 million TVs in the country, for an average of 2.4 per home. American adults watch about 4.6 hours of television per day, or 1,669 hours per year.

Critics ceaselessly point out television's alleged faults. The growing girth of the nation is blamed on it; increased violence; higher levels of teen sexual activity; and finally, we are assured, the idiot box is generally dumbing us all down.

But we have plenty of reasons to doubt that bill of indictment on television. Children today are watching slightly less television per day than they were a decade ago, even as they continue to pork up. Violent crime rates have been falling in the United States for a decade; and rates of teen sexual activity and pregnancy have fallen dramatically since the mid-1990s. Average IQs have been soaring along with TV viewing for decades.

And it's not as though Americans have been sitting in front of their boob tubes and drooling all day for the past half-century of mass TV viewing. Our real gross domestic product has more than quintupled since 1950.

Television Is an Activity

A lot of anti-TV attitudes are based in mere differences of opinion over what qualifies as a judicious use of one's free time. Critics are constantly hectoring viewers to wrench their eyes away from their flickering screens and get out and *do something!* Commentator Nina Buck offers a typical anti-TV screed, claiming that television "steals your life." Buck badgers couch potatoes: "Learn Italian! Take up underwater basket weaving, practice your circus act! Call your grandma, make dinner for your sweetheart, go salsa dancing, use pipe cleaners to make your hair look like Pippi Longstocking's!"

The suggestions are amusing (and I appreciate the tip on how to make my hair look like Pippi Longstocking's), but there is a solemn assumption behind them: that *any* activity will be less wasteful and more edifying than, for example, watching a good episode of *The West Wing*. It's not as though two or three generations ago people were sitting around discussing Kierkegaard and Kant [19th and 18th-century philosophers] with their children over the family dinner table every evening. In fact, most of them were fully engaged in the basic drudgery of earning a living or managing a household. In their scarce leisure time, they might go to a baseball game or read a penny dreadful. In a similar fashion today we might switch on the TV to watch a ball game or an episode of *The Simpsons*.

The New York Times recently described a new survey that reported "what many Americans know but don't always admit, especially to social scientists: that watching TV is a very enjoyable way to pass the time, and that taking care of children—bless their young hearts—is often about as much fun as housework."

All of which is not to say that watching TV does not have some bad aspects—one can always get too much of a good thing—but it is hardly the instrument of mental, cultural, and moral degradation it is so often portrayed as. So feel free to wield that remote from time to time and just relax: There are few things more liberating than doing what you want with your time.

EVALUATING THE AUTHOR'S ARGUMENTS:

The previous viewpoint used an abundance of facts and figures to argue the crucial role that television plays in America's moral degradation. In this viewpoint, Ronald Bailey uses personal and cultural examples to contend that television is not responsible. Which viewpoint do you think presents the strongest case with its form and content?

Viewpoint

5

Reality TV Has Positive Qualities

Ian Wilhelm

"The programs teach that charitable giving is not just the role of the 'super-wealthy.'"

Ian Wilhelm is a reporter who has worked for such publications as *The Chronicle of Philanthropy, Business Publishers, Inc., Community Development Publications*, and *The Baltimore City* Paper. In the following viewpoint, Wilhelm argues that despite its many critics, reality television shows do in fact have positive qualities, one being that these programs offer help to those in need. Wilhelm acknowledges that there have been accusations regarding the shows' potential exploitation for profit, but notes that these shows, more importantly, inspire viewers to help the less fortunate and raise money for charity.

AS YOU READ, CONSIDER THE FOLLOWING QUESTIONS:
1. What does the author suggest is a key part of some reality TV shows' audience appeal?
2. Why do some nonprofit leaders give charity reality shows a negative review?
3. How are several nonprofit groups using the popularity of charity television to educate audiences about their causes?

C harity is coming to the small screen in a big way. The daytime talk-show queen Oprah Winfrey is producing two television shows that will focus on helping needy people, NBC is developing a program in which real-life millionaires will decide how to give away their wealth, and in September [2006], a show sponsored by Nascar, in which mechanics repair beat-up vehicles owned by charity officials and other local leaders, made its debut.

The phenomenon has even crossed the Atlantic. *The Secret Millionaire*, a British series that started broadcasting in October [2006], features a wealthy individual who disguises his or her identity and lives in a working-class area to find a worthy recipient of almost $100,000.

These reality shows, so called because they are unscripted and don't include actors, are part of a growing genre of programs that make doing good—or the appearance of doing good—a key part of their audience appeal.

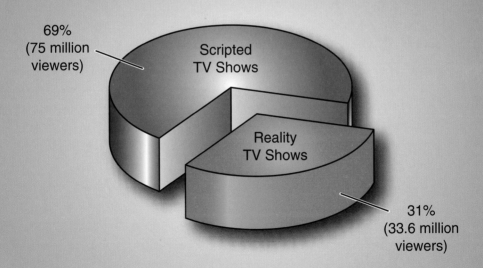

Percentage of Viewers Who Watched Reality vs. Scripted Shows during Fall 2003

69% (75 million viewers)

Scripted TV Shows

Reality TV Shows

31% (33.6 million viewers)

Taken from: Bill Carter, "Networks Find Reality Has Become a Part of Life," New York Times, December 22, 2003

While not all such shows earn high ratings, many Americans are watching them. The most popular, *ABC's Extreme Makeover: Home Edition*, in which a team of builders and designers repair the house of a family in dire economic straits, attracted almost 14 million viewers for a recent episode, making it one of the top 20 most-watched TV programs of that week.

FAST FACT

Reality television accounts for about 56 percent of American TV shows and about 69 percent of world TV shows, according to Nielson Media Research.

Inspiration or Contempt?

The shows are also praised by some scholars and charity officials for inspiring viewers to help the less fortunate and raising money for charitable causes.

Extreme Makeover, for example, has donated part of the proceeds from the sale of its first-season DVD to Habitat for Humanity International, garnering about $50,000 for the Americus, Ga., nonprofit organization.

But some nonprofit leaders give the shows a negative review. They argue the television programs are maudlin [foolishly sentimental] displays of good will, and while a few people may benefit from a rebuilt house or some other windfall, the shows potentially exploit for profit those they try to assist.

Kathryn A. Straniero, executive director of Together We Cope, a social-service organization in Tinley Park, Ill., says she refuses to watch the shows for those reasons.

In America, says Ms. Straniero, "we don't want to put our poor people on display."

To be sure, television shows that entertain by helping others are not new. During the 1950s and '60s, the program *Queen for a Day* had women tell their hard-luck stories to win dishwashers or other prizes.

But today's pack of shows differ from *Queen for a Day*, some observers say, in that they are part of a newfound appreciation for giving in society.

"It's another signal of philanthropy becoming part of the cultural life," says Paul G. Schervish, a professor of sociology and director of

Boston College's Center on Wealth and Philanthropy. The programs teach that charitable giving is not just the role of the 'super-wealthy' he adds. . . .

Charitable Shows Encourage Giving

Indeed, George T. Orfanakos, a charity fund raiser who has been involved with an episode of *Extreme Makeover*, says the show spurs acts of generosity.

Last year, Mr. Orfanakos organized a letter-writing campaign that persuaded the program's producers to help a New Jersey family whose house had burned down. The two-story house, in an impoverished neighborhood in Irvington, was home to several children with physical and emotional disabilities.

A construction company volunteered its services for the rebuilding, which Mr. Orfanakos says cost close to $1-million, and bought the family a van. Such good will represents the spirit that *Extreme Makeover* can engender, says Mr. Orfanakos, who is vice president of development for the Children's Tumor Foundation in New York.

"It brings the best out in people. And for television to do that, thank God, because it's not doing that all the time," he says.

Paige Hemmis, one of *Extreme Makeover's* hosts, says the New Jersey episode was not a fluke.

Many fans write her letters or talk to her at public appearances about what good deeds the show has prompted them to perform, she says.

"Young kids come up and say, 'I mowed my neighbor's grass because he's old,'" she says, laughing at the sweet, but blunt, way children can trumpet their efforts. Ms. Hemmis says she, too, has been motivated by the families she has met during the show's four seasons and is donating a portion of the proceeds from her new home-repair book to Habitat for Humanity.

Some Find Charity Shows Offensive

Yet for all the contributions and volunteers the show may generate, charity as entertainment is a questionable endeavor, say several scholars and nonprofit leaders.

"In the 19th century you used to be able to buy tickets to go to poor houses and watch poor people eat sumptuous Christmas dinners that you helped pay for," says Robert J. Thompson, director of the Center for the Study of Popular Television, at Syracuse University. "The same brain cells are being stimulated in enjoyment as when you watch *Extreme Makeover* and watch a poor family have its house built."

Mr. Thompson does say that today's shows are less offensive than the Dickens-era poverty tourism, in part because they provide desperate people with more than just one meal.

Some social-service leaders refuse to give the shows any slack.

The programs offer "a modest kind of [philanthropy] done for entertainment purposes," says Sheila Crowley, president of the National Low Income Housing Coalition, in Washington. "They're all exploitative."

Lawsuit Over Show

At least one family that has appeared on one of the charity shows agrees. The Higgins family of Southern California—five children who were left orphaned after the death of their parents—in 2005 sued *Extreme Makeover: Home Edition's* producers, charging that they failed to provide them with a new house as promised.

The show did fix up a house for a couple who promised to look after the siblings, who range in age from 15 to 22. But the Higginses allege the caretakers forced them to move out of the home not long after it was refurbished. The couple is also named in the lawsuit.

"Our position is that there's something fundamentally wrong with this whole process," says Patrick A. Mesisca Jr., the lawyer for the Higgins family. He said the children feel exploited by the show.

Extreme Makeover's production company, Endemol USA, in Los Angeles, says it does not comment on lawsuits. In a previous statement to reporters, the couple who housed the Higgins family for a time said the lawsuit was "bogus."

The trial is expected to start in March in the Superior Court of Los Angeles County, says Mr. Mesisca.

While not talking specifically about the lawsuit, Ms. Hemmis, of *Extreme Makeover*, says her show is sensitive to the problem of making caricatures of its beneficiaries.

"If someone says, 'I really don't want anyone knowing this,' or 'This part is really embarrassing, can we leave this quiet?' we always respect that," she says. "Our producers work with the families to make sure they don't feel exploited."

Moreover, *Extreme Makeover: Home Edition* receives more than 1,000 applications a day from families who want to appear on it, a sign that many people believe it treats participants fairly, she says.

'Helping the Helpers'

In part because of the concern about exploitation, though, at least one charity TV program, *Nascar Angels*, has shifted its focus away from helping people in economic crisis to helping charity officials, teachers, and other local leaders, while also teaching general automotive skills to viewers.

In the show, the racing legend Rusty Wallace travels the country to fix beat-up vehicles owned by good Samaritans. The pilot episode, which never aired, featured a victim of domestic violence, but "there was a concern about, is it going to be the poor-person-of-the-week show," says Phil Alvidrez, the program's producer. The show is now primarily focused on "helping the helpers," he explains.

He says the show's goal is to provide practical upgrades to vehicles. "It's not so much *Pimp My Ride* but to make them really serviceable and safe," he says, referring to an MTV show that transforms jalopies [old, worn out automobiles] into flashy roadsters.

For instance, on a recent episode of *Nascar Angels*, mechanics made several thousand dollars worth of repairs to a 1990 Volkswagen van for Mary Setterholm, the leader of L.A. Surf Bus, a charity in Hermosa Beach, Calif., that teaches inner-city youths about the ocean and how to surf.

In her old van, "I was lucky to go 20 miles per hour up any hill," she says. Now with her new vehicle, which she has nicknamed "Miracle II," the former women's surfing champion can carry her equipment and doesn't have to worry about the doors literally falling off.

Her appearance also has made her a minor celebrity. "I get stopped all the time. I had one guy definitely hit on me," she says, laughing.

Inspiring Gifts

For other charities that appear on philanthropic [providing charitable assistance] TV programs, the national exposure can lead to more tangible benefits.

For example, Autism Speaks, a New York charity, raised more than

$113,000 thanks to an appearance on *The Apprentice* in December 2005, says Alison T. Singer, the organization's senior vice president.

The Apprentice, in which contestants compete for a job with Donald Trump [an American business executive], is not strictly about philanthropy, but Mr. Trump stresses that charitable giving is part of running a successful business and ends each season with fund-raising efforts.

In the show's fourth season, Randal Pinkett, a contestant on the show, organized a celebrity softball game in Brooklyn for Autism Speaks.

The game was rained out, but Mr. Pinkett impressed Mr. Trump and others by making an impassioned plea for more scientific research and public advocacy efforts to help children afflicted with the disease.

"He got up at the event and he spoke from the heart as if he had been an autism advocate for his entire life," says Ms. Singer. "He really was an autism rock star on *The Apprentice*."

The group, which was co-founded two years ago by the chief execu-

Some reality shows have a positive impact on people like this family whose home was rebuilt for an epsiode of Extreme Makeover: Home Edition.

tive officer of NBC Universal, garnered $61,000 during the event and once the episode aired, viewers donated additional funds through the charity's Web site.

What's more, Mr. Pinkett, who ultimately won the show, continues to be a national spokesman for the group.

Charity Shows Ignore Causes of Social Ills

While becoming a partner with a reality show paid off for Autism Speaks, one scholar raises concerns that the programs indirectly convey a message to the American public that may hurt charities in the long run.

Eric Bain-Selbo, associate professor of religion and philosophy at Lebanon Valley College, in Annville, Pa., worries that the newly popular Hollywood "noblesse oblige" can overshadow what he sees as the government's responsibility to aid its citizens.

In the case of *Extreme Makeover: Home Edition*, "you build a brand-new home for families, but you completely miss the larger social questions that underlie why this family needs this show to come in for them," he says.

While he acknowledges that the television industry's goal is to entertain, not to solve the nation's problems, he would like to know more about the people who are assisted on the show.

"Is there a lack of high-paying manufacturing jobs in the region, so the father's out of work?" he asks. "Is there unequal access to higher education so that members of the family have never been able to get the training or the education to get higher-paying jobs? Is there an inadequate health-care system and that's why the family's in crisis because they cannot maintain the upkeep on the home because they have a kid who is sick?"

Beyond Social Services

Perhaps with these concerns in mind, several nonprofit groups are using the popularity of charity television to confront broader social ills.

The American Civil Liberties Union, in New York, and the Sierra Club, in San Francisco, in the last two years [prior to 2007] have created 30-minute shows that feature everyday people fighting for the causes those groups promote.

The documentary-style programs lack the game-show feel of, say,

Extreme Makeover, and have a smaller potential number of viewers than the commercial programs, but both organizations consider them a valuable way to educate Americans about their social concerns.

For example, the ACLU says its video preview of the show on its Web site is watched on average by 22,000 Internet viewers a month.

Along with these two national groups, at least one local charity also has become a part-time television producer.

The D.C. Central Kitchen is creating a reality show that will feature the ex-convicts, former drug addicts, and other hardscrabble people it trains to be cooks.

Robert Egger, president of the Washington charity, says the program could educate viewers about the plight of the poor and the benefits of healthy eating, while also providing a little drama as the students navigate their new responsibilities.

"Part of the show would really give us the ability for someone to say, My name's Reginald. I've been in prison for 20 years, I'm really trying to get myself together now, and I'm learning a skill. Today I'm going to help you learn how to cook with fennel," he says.

The show just started to air on a Washington cable channel, but Mr. Egger hopes to find a national outlet for it or a similar TV program.

So far, though, television executives haven't fully grasped the concept, Mr. Egger says.

In response to his idea, they often say, "We love it, man, we can't wait to do it—but we just can't figure out who gets voted out of the kitchen."

The reaction perhaps is a larger sign of the challenge any television program faces when mixing charity and entertainment.

"How do you find the nice middle ground?" Mr. Egger asks. "This is the conundrum."

EVALUATING THE AUTHOR'S ARGUMENTS:

In the viewpoint you just read, author Ian Wilhelm argues that reality TV shows offer help to those less fortunate while both entertaining and inspiring audiences. In the following viewpoint, Howard Rosenberg calls the current reality TV trend "depressingly lean and ugly." After reading both viewpoints and considering your own personal experiences watching reality TV shows, with which argument do you agree? Give your reasons.

"Reality" Television Does Not Have Positive Qualities

Howard Rosenberg

"Real, my eye. Moreover, calling these shows 'unscripted,' as many do, is also misleading, implying a level of naturalness not present."

Howard Rosenberg is a now-retired TV columnist for the *Los Angeles Times.* In 1985, he won a Pulitzer Prize for criticism. In the following viewpoint, Rosenberg argues that in addition to oversaturating the market, reality shows are deceiving viewers: they do not reflect any form of reality, in Rosenberg's opinion. They are scripted, for one thing, and heavily edited, he argues. The "reality" label is similar to deceptive language used in other forms of media, especially advertising, Rosenberg contends, and is unfair to viewers.

AS YOU READ, CONSIDER THE FOLLOWING QUESTIONS:
1. What television era does Rosenberg identify as being as equally deficient in quality as today?

2. What was the first "break-out" reality show, according to the author?

3. How does Rosenberg use the word *euphemism* in the viewpoint?

If ever television needed an extreme makeover, it's now. Sorry, FCC [Federal Communications Commission], but the problem is more onerous than the likes of Janet Jackson, Bono, or even Howard Stern. It's not a peekaboo boob here, not so-called smut nor the f-word. It's the dreaded r-word.

"Reality."

Arrrrrrgh!

From *Survivor* to its many progeny swimming like tadpoles in the media stream, "reality" is the Bethlehem star for this millennium's TV programmers. As [the 2004] summer and . . . fall season reaffirm, their eyes light up like slot machines when sighting a show concept with "reality" potential, which to them can cover anything from sports to spot welding.

Rouging these shows up to make them appear different doesn't alter the fact that they're essentially breaking old ground, again and again.

And that "reality" label? Get real.

Reality TV Is Unoriginal

The industry sees profit in it, however speciously it's applied. In 2002's *The Hamptons,* for example, ABC gave us TV's "first reality miniseries," which in earlier years would have been called a documentary. And TBS labeled its *Worst-Case Scenario* TV's first "reality" magazine series, as if *60 Minutes* never existed.

This is not another lament hemorrhaging praise for the "golden age" of TV, which only amnesiacs stubbornly insist was all that golden. In limited ways, in fact, TV's present entertainment profile is handsomer than ever, thanks largely to original programming by HBO and improving Showtime.

FAST FACT

One of the earliest unscripted television shows depicting real people was *Candid Camera* in 1948.

Some people feel that reality shows like American Idol are contrived and lack originality.

Nor are TV copycats a new phenomenon. Like feature films and theater, the small screen has regenerated itself for generations, its DNA dictating that hot shows beget sequels or be copied in quadruplicate with ratings in mind.

Yet we're in a period now that is depressingly lean, and ugly, for those who treasure originality in entertainment.

TV has not been as derivative en masse since the 1950s and early 1960s when first quiz shows and then Westerns thundered across prime time like buffalo herds. In 2004, creativity is again limited to the occasional tumbleweed.

Reality TV Is Oversaturated

Survivor creator Mark Burnett is widely seen as the godfather of "reality." Not so. The genre was seeded in the 1973 PBS series *An American Family*, which kept a close-up lens on the Loud family of Santa Barbara, Calif., for weeks, and, arguably, even earlier in the fly-on-the-wall films of Fred Wiseman and other documentarians whose cinema verité cameras discovered fascination in life's routine. Though not always successful, their goal was art. Now come the low-enders.

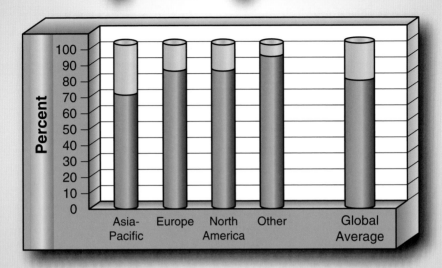

Since the break-out success of *Survivor in* 2000, shows labeled "reality" have surfaced like measles spots. Think glut, with the wheels on this bandwagon now buckling. Nearly everyone is hopping on, from O.J. Simpson, who told an interviewer he's ready to join the game, to TV producer David E. Kelley, who interrupted his criticism of the genre long enough to sign a "reality" show deal with NBC.

I began tallying the "reality" shows airing across TV just this summer [of 2004] and stopped when I hit 20 because my eyes had glazed over. They range from golden oldies like *Big Brother 5* on CBS and *Joe Schmo 2* on Spike TV to at least a dozen newcomers.

You get hairdresser "reality" in Bravo's *Blow Out*, high-stakes "reality" in The Discovery Channel's *American Casino* and Fox's *The Casino*. You get tightly wound brides "reality" in WE's *Bridezillas*, Aussie hubba-hubba "reality" in a dozen babes competing for a hunk on TBS's *Outback Jack*. You get election "reality" in Showtime's *American Candidate*, mobster's daughter "reality" in A&E's *Growing Up Gotti*. And so on and so on. . . .

All of them so real you can hardly stand it.

The Word "Reality" Is Inaccurate

My most recent dose of this bracing realism came in tuning in *The Ultimate Love Test* on ABC and witnessing beautiful "reality" faces pour their hearts out (poor babies) about relationships and romance with a $100,000 payday in their crosshairs. They were so honest, so candid, so spontaneous. With cameras on their noses, TV cable at their feet, and production crews at their sides. To say nothing of "reality" tweaking, courtesy of the editing room.

Real, my eye. Moreover, calling these shows "unscripted," as many do, is also misleading, implying a level of naturalness not present.

Much of advertising is underpinned by wordspin, from real estate agents promoting rickety houses as "needing tender loving care" to used cars sold as "pre-owned." TV has its own slippery tongue, regularly deploying euphemisms in selling products and itself, as in calling reruns "encore" episodes, implying they're back by public demand. The next step would be to call them "pre-seen."

It's "reality," however, that earns quotation marks as TV's overused, misused word of the century. The longer it's applied to shows that are largely faux, the more viewers will become desensitized and accept them as genuine.

EVALUATING THE AUTHOR'S ARGUMENTS:

Howard Rosenberg, author of the viewpoint you just read, takes a generally negative view of reality television programming. One of his specific complaints is that producers are deceiving viewers by not revealing that the shows are somewhat scripted and highly edited. Do you think that producers should reveal how much of the show is "real" and how much is "planned," and were this to happen, would your view of reality television change? Why or why not?

Chapter 3

Who Should Control Television?

Many people debate whether the government should take responsibility for regulating television content or if it should fall to the networks or even the consumer.

Networks Should Take Responsibility for Harmful Television Content

Michael Tracey

"Why wait for regulators? Why not establish voluntary restrictions on what advertising is aimed, through [the TV networks], at young children?"

Michael Tracey is a professor of journalism and mass communication at the University of Colorado at Boulder. The following viewpoint is excerpted from an open letter Tracey wrote to the general managers of the three major television networks (ABC, CBS, and NBC) in Denver, Colorado. Tracey contends that the networks themselves should take responsibility for the content they broadcast. In self-limiting harmful content such as unhealthy food commercials and violence in programs, Tracey argues, the networks will be fulfilling their duty to the community as well as protecting the emotional well-being of children.

AS YOU READ, CONSIDER THE FOLLOWING QUESTIONS:

1. How much do advertisers spend on messages aimed at the young, according to Tracey?
2. What did the APA's team of psychologists find with regard to children and television advertising, as reported by the author?
3. What two voluntary limitations does the author recommend the networks implement?

Gentlemen,

As general managers of the three major network affiliate stations in Denver you carry an enormous responsibility to this community, a responsibility I know you treat with the utmost seriousness. I therefore wanted to draw your attention to a new report of which you may not be aware. The American Psychological Association in 2000 appointed a task force of experts from a range of disciplines

New technologies, like the V-chip, allow consumers to control the kind of content they allow to be viewed on their televisions.

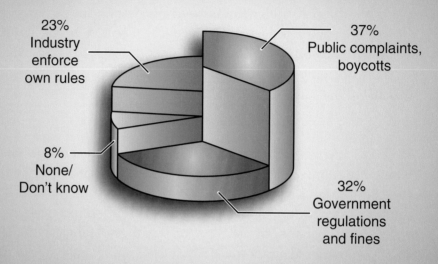

The Most Effective Remedies for Media Sex and Violence, People Believe

23%
Industry
enforce
own rules

37%
Public complaints,
boycotts

8%
None/
Don't know

32%
Government
regulations
and fines

Taken from: Pew Research Center, "Support for Tougher Indecency Measures, But Worries About Government Intrusiveness," April 15, 2005

to look into the issue of advertising to young children. Their report, *Advertising and Children,* was recently published.

It is estimated that advertisers spend more than $12 billion per year on advertising messages aimed at the young. Additionally, the average child watches more than 40,000 television commercials per year. That's a lot of television.

The APA's six-member team of psychologists with expertise in child development, cognitive psychology and social psychology found that children under the age of 8 lack the cognitive development to understand the persuasive intent of television advertising and are uniquely susceptible to advertising's influence. Because of this "they are easy targets for commercial persuasion," said psychologist Brian Wilcox, Ph.D., professor of psychology and director of the Center on Children, Families and the Law at the University of Nebraska and chairman of the task force.

In other words, young children are vulnerable and open to manipulation. Wilcox adds: "This is a critical concern because the most common products marketed to children are sugared cereals, candies, sweets, sodas and snack foods. Such advertising of unhealthy food products to young children contributes to poor nutritional habits that might last a lifetime and be a variable in the current epidemic of obesity among kids."

The report also expressed concerns about such things as young children seeing ads for beer that were intended for adults but that unintentionally nurture positive attitudes towards drinking in kids as young as 9. They also point to concerns about ads that sell violence, whether in movies or video games. The report quotes research that suggests that even young children readily recall the content of ads to which they have been exposed.

Their conclusion is to urge federal regulators to restrict advertising to children 8 years old and younger, and to examine other ways in which children of all ages can be protected from what the authors— clearly with passion—believe to be the seriously negative consequences of advertising for the young.

It's here that I thought I would write to you since you and I both know that there is more chance of the University of Colorado football program being nominated for the Nobel Peace Prize than there is of the Federal Communications Commission or Congress or the White House agreeing to such restrictions.

My question to you gentlemen is: Why wait for the regulators? Why not establish voluntary restrictions on what advertising is aimed, through your station, at young children? You have seen the reports that obesity, according to Dr. Julie Gerberding, director of the Centers for Disease Control and Prevention, is now the fastest-growing health crisis in the industrialized world; that nearly 9 million children in America are affected; and that Type II diabetes, an obesity-linked disorder once seen only in adults, is now increasingly common in children.

You may have read the comment by Professor Ellen Ruppert Shell, of Boston University's Knight Center for Science and Medical Journalism that "children are bombarded with junk-food advertising on television crafted to persuade them that free choice in life is simply a matter of whether to supersize their Value Meals."

Living in Colorado, you are also intimately familiar with the problems of violence among the young, violence which the APA suggests is linked to the selling of violence through advertising which naturalizes it, makes it more acceptable and "normal."

Therefore, let me suggest that you establish a 9 p.m. watershed, before which you would:

Voluntarily ban all advertising of foodstuffs the consumption of which would tend to create poor physical specimens;

Voluntarily ban all advertising for products that are characterized by violent acts;

Voluntarily restrict any and all advertising aimed at the truly young—the APA uses 8 years old or younger;

Consult with parents, teachers, community leaders, child psychologists, children on how they feel television might help nurture the young rather than, in effect, abuse them.

I understand that not all society's ills are caused by television, any more than they can be solved by television. But you can offer powerful concrete and symbolic leadership. It will cost you, I realize, but what is more important—the psychological, emotional and educational well-being of children or your profit margin? And if you have to even pause to think how to answer that question then that does suggest that this society really is in deep doo-doo.

EVALUATING THE AUTHOR'S ARGUMENTS:

Michael Tracey chose to write his article, which was published in a local newspaper, in the form of a letter to the managers of the networks in his city. He asks these managers to voluntarily restrict content on their broadcasts that may be harmful to children. What effect does the format of the article—a letter—have on the author's argument? Do you think the letter format makes Tracey's argument more or less effective? Explain.

Parents Should Take Responsibility for Harmful Television Content

Adam Thierer

> "*Parents need to act responsibly and exercise their private right . . . to censor their children's eyes and ears from certain things.*"

Adam Thierer is the director of telecommunications at the Cato Institute, a libertarian nonprofit policy research organization that works to protect the free market and limit government. In the following viewpoint, Thierer argues that it is not the responsibility of the government nor of the networks to control harmful television content, but rather it is the duty of parents to protect their children from material that might not be appropriate. People need to take personal responsibility, he contends, rather than depending on the government to censor material, which he sees as undermining the principles of a free society.

One of my earliest memories involves watching a monster movie on TV. I seem to recall it involved zombies hiding in a closet and grabbing people as they entered the room. Pretty creepy stuff and, quite honestly, I probably should not have been watching it. I'm not sure what mom was doing at the time, but she probably should have turned the TV off or found something better for me to watch.

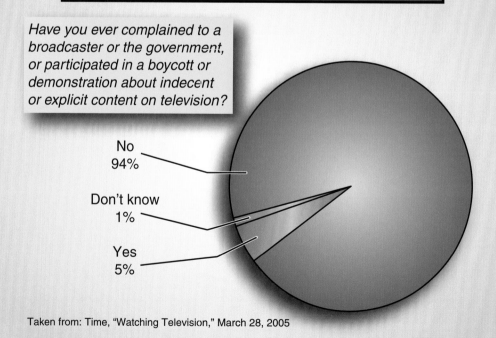

Most Americans Have Not Complained About Television Content

Have you ever complained to a broadcaster or the government, or participated in a boycott or demonstration about indecent or explicit content on television?

No
94%

Don't know
1%

Yes
5%

Taken from: Time, "Watching Television," March 28, 2005

If we are to believe some members of Congress, however, exposure to such violent images should have turned me into a madman. But even though I went on to watch more violent movies and programs, last time I checked, I still hadn't harmed or killed anyone. Like millions of other kids

who grew up watching cowboy shoot-em-ups, weekend "creature features," or just plain old cops-and-robbers crime dramas, I learned how to separate fantasy from reality. Are there some unstable kids out there who are negatively influenced by violent images on TV? Sure. But one wonders how big that population really is and whether the root cause of their problems lies elsewhere (bad homes, bad neighborhoods, or even serious mental conditions). The academic literature is all over the place on this question, and debates still rage about correlation versus causation when it comes to violent programming and aggressive behavior.

Parents Need to Be Responsible

Regardless, our knights in shining armor in Congress are once again proposing to ride to our collective rescue and sanitize television "for the sake of the children." The "for the children" mantra has quickly become the universal pretext for legislative attempts to censor TV, radio, cable, video games and the Internet. Apparently, if you have the best interests of children in mind, you can dispense with the First Amendment and let the government censor whatever it pleases.

Maybe I sound like a broken record for posing this question in every essay on censorship I pen, but I'm going to go ahead and ask it again: What ever happened to personal and parental responsibility in this country? The responses I get generally fall into one of two camps. One group says personal responsibility died a slow but certain death in this country a long time ago and that I'm just another principled but quixotic dreamer who has yet to come to grips with the inevitability of government censorship. This group doesn't like the sound of censorship, but is apparently willing to live with it, or they've just given up fighting the good fight. Another group, however, openly embraces the idea of Uncle Sam playing the role of surrogate parent in our homes. They lament the fact that media is so ubiquitous in our lives today and say they've largely given up trying to keep tabs on what their kids watch or listen to.

Either way, a lot of people appear ready to raise the white flag and let government censor "for the children." So the censorship crusade du jour, aimed at getting "excessive violence" out of the media, suddenly seems like a very real possibility. The Senate included a measure in a military spending bill (how's that for irony!) that would ban violent video programming on broadcast TV during hours in which children might be in the audience (basically anytime before 10:00 p.m.). And 39 members of the House Commerce Committee wrote to the FCC [Federal Communications Commission] requesting that the agency study what it could do about violence on television. The FCC quickly responded by announcing a new inquiry into the issue. Meanwhile, there are still lurking threats of regulation of supposedly overly violent video games at both the federal and state levels.

Violence Is Present in the Media

But while the censorship bandwagon is really rolling [in 2004] in the wake of the Janet Jackson incident [at the Super Bowl halftime show], I would hope there are a few brave souls left out there willing to fight attempts by Beltway [Washington, D.C.,] bureaucrats to dictate what our families can see or hear. The fundamental problem with proposals to censor violence in media is that they will require that the government make myriad "eye of the beholder" decisions about what is "too violent" on behalf of all Americans. Choices that we should be making voluntarily for ourselves and our children are suddenly choices made through the political process, with its coercive ability to silence any views or content it finds unacceptable.

Consider the ramifications of allowing a handful of folks down at the FCC to determine what constitutes "excessive violence." Are the bloody and occasionally gruesome scenes in CSI and ER excessive, or is that a reasonable depiction of forensic and medical science? Hockey games on prime-time TV feature lots of fights, blood, and lost teeth. For decades, cartoons have offered a buffet of violent acts, and slapstick comedy of the Three Stooges variety features a lot of unforgivingly violent moments presented as humor. Should regula-

Many people would like television networks and video game companies to be more accountable for their content, which may include realistic violence that may be inappropriate for children.

tors also censor the many combat-oriented video games on the market today that involve extremely realistic military training and war game scenarios, some of which even rely on the consulting services of former military officials? How about gruesome war scenes from actual combat that any child can see on the nightly news? What about the stabbing, poisoning, and other heinous acts found in Shakespeare's tragedies? And, for God's sake (excuse the pun), what about all the violence in the Bible or Mel Gibson's *The Passion of the Christ?*

Parents vs. Government
I could go on and on, but you get the point. This all comes down to a question of who calls the shots—parents or government—regarding

what we are allowed to see and hear in a free society. This is not to say society must celebrate or even defend violence in the media; there are plenty of movies, shows and games that do contain what many parents would regard as a troubling amount of violent content for young children to witness. Parents need to act responsibly and exercise their private right—indeed, responsibility—to censor their children's eyes and ears from certain things. It's become increasingly evident, however, that a lot of parents have just gotten lazy about carrying out

Motion Picture Association of America President, Jack Valenti, announcing the television ratings systems designed to help parents choose which programs are appropriate for their children.

this difficult job. While I can appreciate the hassle of constantly trying to monitor a child's viewing and listening habits, that's no excuse for throwing in the towel and calling in the government to censor what the rest of the world has access to.

By the way, let's not forget that we long ago opened the door to government censorship when we allowed them to mandate that those silly "V-Chips" be installed in every TV set to supposedly help us censor sex and violence. Have you ever met anyone who uses them? Neither have I, but many lawmakers will use that fact as yet another reason to censor more directly. Those who were ridiculed for predicting that the V-Chip could lead to more far-reaching censorship of violence on television deserve an apology.

Finally, one wonders what all this hand-wringing over violence means for cable and satellite programs and providers. This has been a watershed year [i.e., 2004] in terms of congressional attempts to assert control over content on pay TV, with several proposals flying to "do something" about indecency on cable. And now the Senate wants to regulate violence on cable too, although it is willing to carve out "premium" or pay-per-view services. Thus, *The Sopranos* gets a pass while *Nip/Tuck* and *The Shield* are apparently fair game for the censors. All because the Senate argues that "broadcast television, cable television and video programming are uniquely pervasive presences in the lives of all American children, and (are) readily accessible to all American children." Again, it's all "for the children." But is there anyone left in government who will stand up for freedom, the First Amendment, and personal responsibility?

EVALUATING THE AUTHOR'S ARGUMENTS:

There are many opinions on who should control what children see on television. The authors of the two preceding viewpoints, Tracey and Thierer, offered different points of view: networks should control what children see and parents should control what children see. After looking back over these viewpoints, which argument do you agree with the most? Why?

Cable Channel Choice Should Be Permitted

Martha Kleder

"'A la carte' pricing, the free market solution, would give consumers complete control over what comes into their homes."

Martha Kleder is a policy analyst for the conservative family-values organization Concerned Women for America. In the following viewpoint, Kleder argues that instead of being forced to buy bundles of cable channels, the government should force cable companies to offer "a la carte" channels to consumers, so that consumers can pick the specific ones they want to watch. Under the current situation, Kleder notes, consumers are forced to pay for channels they consider indecent or obscene, which cable companies include because they attract viewers. The free market should be permitted to decide which channels will survive and which will not, she argues, and under the current system, this is not possible.

AS YOU READ, CONSIDER THE FOLLOWING QUESTIONS:
1. In the opinion of the author, why did cable networks begin "pushing the bounds of decency?"

2. What evidence does Kleder give of cable companies' monopoly on local communities?
3. What three ways does the author say that a la carte choices will encourage companies to improve their services?

I f viewers are told to "just change channels" when they don't want certain programs, then they should not be forced to purchase those unwanted programs in a bundled package.

The average cable customer watches only 12 to 15 channels on a regular basis, but cable companies bundle 50 to 75 channels in the basic tier, and upwards of 200 in digital cable packages. That's like going to the store for a dozen eggs and being told you must buy at least six dozen.

This forced consumption of channels increases the cost to consumers. A Federal Communications Commission (FCC) report concludes that

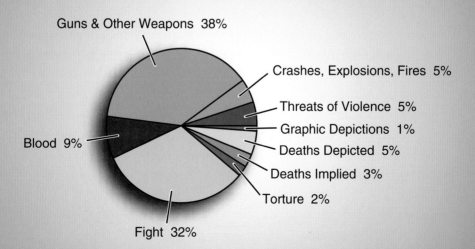

Types of Violence on Television

Violent Content by Type During the Family Hour - 2002

Guns & Other Weapons 38%
Crashes, Explosions, Fires 5%
Threats of Violence 5%
Graphic Depictions 1%
Deaths Depicted 5%
Blood 9%
Deaths Implied 3%
Torture 2%
Fight 32%

Taken from: Parents Television Council, "TV Bloodbath: Violence on Prime Time Broadcast TV," 2003

cable subscription prices have increased five times faster than the rate of inflation.

Under the cable bundling system, even non-sports fans are forced to pay for very costly programming such as ESPN. Sports fans, too, face higher cable bills because of channel bundling.

"A la carte" pricing, the free market solution, would give consumers complete control over what comes into their homes and would help them control their cable bills.

While being content-neutral in wording and goals, such a plan could also reduce the amount of indecent programming, as families vote with their pocketbooks.

Cable TV Contains Indecent Material

Cable networks are not bound by broadcast indecency statutes. So when some cable networks began producing their own programs, they used raw, sexualized content to draw viewers.

Broadcasters then began pushing the bounds of decency in an attempt to reclaim those viewers. "We have to compete with cable" is an excuse voiced frequently in entertainment periodicals. However, a close look at the parent companies of these cable channels shows that, in large part, they are owned by the same conglomerates that own the broadcast networks.

Gail Berman, Fox Entertainment president, told Gannett News Service in October 2002 that the racy cop show *Fastlane* was added to their broadcast line-up because, "[W]e must be able to compete with *The Shield.*" *The Shield*, another crude and highly controversial police drama, airs on FX, a Fox-owned channel on the basic cable tier.

The idea of "competition" between cable and network TV is also undone by the fact that many themes, and even programs, have crossed from cable to network.

MTV gave us *Real World* and *Jackass* several years ago. Now, broadcast TV features shows like *Big Brother* and *Fear Factor.* Bravo pre-

Some people would prefer to choose cable channels that support their values rather than being forced to subscribe to channels with content like The Sopranos, which viewers may feel is too violent.

miered *Queer Eye for the Straight Guy*, which now runs on its sister broadcast network, NBC. The list of crossover themes and programs grows with each program cycle.

Ultimate blame for this race to the bottom lies with the FCC's lack of indecency enforcement. The FCC's inaction has blurred the lines between broadcast and cable.

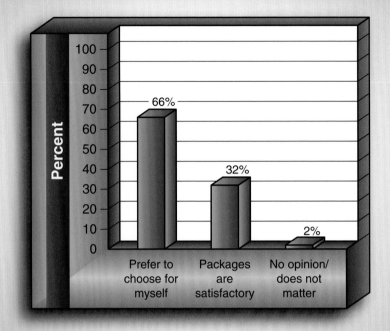

Taken from: Concerned Women for America, "Cable Choice Is Channel Choice," April 2004

Cable Companies Hold Monopoly Power

Over 94 million homes subscribe to multichannel video programming distributors (MVPDs), according to an FCC report. Of those, about 66 million subscribe to cable while the remainder subscribe to direct broadcast satellite (DBS). The number of MVPD subscriber homes accounts for 88.29 percent of all television households.

While there are about a dozen major cable companies nationwide, those companies act as monopolies in their local communities, by county charter.

Satellite systems, while starting to nibble at cable's customer base, are not yet a true competitor, and thus have no direct impact on cable prices. As Gene Kimmelman of Consumers Union notes, the cable industry is 3.5 times larger than dish systems, many DBS customers live where cable is not available, and dish placement restrictions prevent many customers from choosing that system over cable.

Along with producing the programming, media conglomerates also hold sway over cable and DBS providers in strict carriage contracts. Those contracts set the price of programming, which is steadily increasing, and also determine channel and tier placement, leaving cable operators with little discretion.

It's time for cable television to come of age and enter the free market.

Cable choice will improve cable services by:

- Encouraging creation of channels that cater to their target audience.
- Phasing out unpopular and redundant channels that drive up cable costs.
- Allowing customers to bear the cost only of the programs they watch.
- Facilitating a more direct financial impact on channels that violate the viewer's standards of decency.

Don't want THEIR MTV? Don't pay for it.

Cable choice lets the free market work its magic, and it just might help clean up the airwaves.

EVALUATING THE AUTHOR'S ARGUMENTS:

The author of the viewpoint you just read, Martha Kleder, and the author of the following viewpoint, David Cohen, disagree about how cable channels should be offered to consumers. Both state, however, that the free market has decided in his or her favor. After reading both viewpoints, which do you think the free market has favored? Support your answer with evidence from the viewpoints.

Cable Channel Choice Should Not Be Permitted

David L. Cohen

"An a la carte regime would guarantee that there will be fewer program-ming choices and less diversity."

David L. Cohen is the executive vice president of the Comcast Corporation, a cable and media company. The following viewpoint is excerpted from testimony Cohen gave before the Senate Committee on Commerce, Science, and Transportation. Cohen presents the argument that if the government permitted consumers to pick and choose their cable channels, called "a la carte" pricing, the industry, diversity, and the market would suffer. Cable companies must offer cable packages in order to survive competition from other companies, Cohen argues. In addition, small, ethnic cable channels rely on packages to bring their programs to viewers. In addition, Cohen reminds the committee, the choice should be made by the free market not by the government, and in his opinion the market has decided against a la carte pricing.

David L. Cohen, "Prepared Statement of David L. Cohen Before The United States Senate Committee On Commerce, Science and Transportation," in commerce.senate.gov, January 19, 2006.

AS YOU READ, CONSIDER THE FOLLOWING QUESTIONS:
1. According to Cohen, what are the three basic laws a la carte pricing would violate if implemented?
2. Why would a la carte pricing harm niche ethnic channels, in the author's opinion?
3. To what other societal institution does Cohen compare cable channel packaging?

America's cable companies deeply value our relationship with our customers. We want to provide them with the greatest possible choice and control. At the same time, we want to run our businesses in a sound economic manner so that we can deliver the advanced services that our customers want and deserve.

Today, Americans have access to a dizzying array of video and interactive media choices. There is something for every possible taste. But not *everything* in the marketplace is to *everyone's* taste.

As the nation's largest cable company, Comcast is sincerely committed to ensure that our customers have all the choice they want, and all the controls they need. So, as some have asked for more alternatives to help manage family viewing, we have listened to them.

We have to deal with a few practical constraints, including the laws of economics, contracts and physics. We need to make decisions that are economically sensible for us and for the companies that provide content to us. We must honor our contractual agreements. And we need to come up with approaches that meet the needs of both our digital cable customers and of our customers who use analog cable equipment.

FAST FACT

The FCC's indecency regulations do not extend to cable-only programming.

A la Carte Cable Will Not Work

While some consumer groups have advocated that cable and satellite companies be required to make all of their channels available on an a la carte basis, this would violate the laws of economics, contracts, and physics.

Some people fear that niche cable channels focusing on specific interests would suffer if consumers could purchase individual channels instead of packages.

First, a la carte services cannot be delivered to analog cable set-top boxes. To offer a la carte would require the individual sale of all of our channels, which would mean that 100 percent of television sets in cable homes would have to be equipped with digital set-top boxes. At the current state of technology, this would be prohibitively expensive for us and for our customers.

Second, we have scores of complex programming contracts in which cable networks have negotiated for the right to be carried on specified tiers of cable service. In an a la carte world, all of these contracts would have to be unwound or abrogated by force of law. This would be hugely disruptive to our industries, extremely expensive, and undoubtedly exceedingly litigious.

Third, after imposing all of those unnecessary costs and complications, an a la carte regime would yield no consumer benefits. Every independent analysis that has been conducted . . . has concluded that an a la carte regime would lead to consumers paying more and getting less.

A la Carte Would Harm Diversity

An a la carte regime would guarantee that there will be fewer programming choices and less diversity. Over 200 consumer and civil rights organizations, elected officials, and others have gone on record objecting to the devastating effects that a mandatory a la carte regime would have on programming diversity. Dozens of creators of niche networks, who know their success depends on their ability to reach the greatest possible number of women, or African-Americans, or Hispanic-Americans, or other specialized segments, have protested that a la carte would sound their death knell.

Many analogies have been used to explain why a la carte is a bad idea. I think the most compelling analogy is to a public library. All of us pay for the maintenance of our libraries. Each library contains thousands and thousands of volumes. Most people will never open most of those volumes, but someone is likely to look at every volume at some point. If we cared only about the volumes that most people wanted to read most of the time, our libraries would look like *The New York Times* best-seller list. But none of us would want to sacrifice the immense diversity that our libraries contain, and all of us benefit from the opportunity to browse and to find something that we didn't know about before.

Cable and satellite television work much the same way. Everyone pays about the same for basic service, and these fees (plus advertising sales) help to support an incredible diversity of programming. Not everyone who watches cable watches every channel, of course. But this economic model, which puts scores of channels into customers' homes, is a proven success.

The Market Has Decided Against a la Carte

If an a la carte regime were pro-consumer, then surely one of the numerous competitors in the marketplace . . . would have adopted that model by now to distinguish themselves from their competitors. The fact that none of these companies has seriously pursued an a la carte model speaks volumes about the lack of viability of this concept in the marketplace. . . .

Every hour of every day, we compete for our customers' loyalty against [other cable companies] as they offer competing cable services. To succeed, we must offer our customers choice, control, convenience and good value. We want parents to think of us as their partners. We want to offer every home the widest possible range of video programming, but we also want to give them the power to tailor their selections for the unique needs of each household.

We always remain open to constructive ideas about ways to better serve our customers. We think the competition we all face in the multichannel television marketplace compels all of us to keep our eyes and ears wide open.

EVALUATING THE AUTHOR'S ARGUMENTS:

In the viewpoint you just read, David Cohen compares cable channels packaged in bundles to a public library, arguing that everyone pays for all the books in a library but no one person reads every book. In your opinion, is this a fair comparison? How is cable television different from a library? How is it the same? Use evidence from your own experiences to support your answer.

Facts About Television

Television Globally
- The first demonstration of a working television system was in 1926 at the London laboratory of engineer John Logic Baird.
- The United Kingdom was the first country in the world to receive television in homes, beginning in 1936.
- One of the last countries in the world to receive television services was the South Asian country of Bhutan in 1995.

Television in the United States
- Researcher Gregory Fouts reports that over three-fourths of the female characters in TV sitcoms are underweight and only one in twenty are above average in size.

According to the nonprofit organization The Television Project:

- 66 percent of Americans eat dinner while watching television.
- Americans collectively spend 231 billion hours per year watching television.
- The average adult, by age sixty-five, will have spent nine years watching television.

Television Advertising
- Television advertising hit its peak in 2004, when the industry spent 9 billion dollars. In the years since, TV advertising has declined, reports the *Christian Science Monitor*.
- The American Psychological Association has found that children under the age of eight are unable to critically understand television advertising and will accept what they see in commercials as true.
- According to the American Academy of Pediatrics, television advertising directly contributes to obesity, poor nutrition, and cigarette and alcohol use among American youth.

Children and Television
- Over half of American children have a television in their bedrooms, according to a 2006 report from the Kaiser Family Foundation.

- According to Nielsen Media Research, teenagers aged twelve to seventeen watched 3 percent more television in 2006 than in 2004–2005. Children aged two to eleven watched 4 percent more.
- According to the Media Awareness Network, the average North American girl will spend five thousand hours watching television before she starts kindergarten.
- According to the Pew Research Center, parents are more concerned about what their children see on the Internet (73 percent) than on television (61 percent). With the Internet, parents' greatest concern is child predators, whereas with television, the greatest concern is that children spend too much time watching it.

Television, Race, and Ethnicity

According to Nielsen Media Research:
- The television is on in the homes of African Americans seventy-nine hours per week, as compared with fifty-two hours per week in white homes.
- Black children watched two more hours of television per day than do white children.
- In 2006, Hispanic households watched seventeen hours of television per week, as compared with thirteen hours in all U.S. households. In addition, the number of Hispanic households that had televisions increased by 12 percent from 2003 to 2005.

Government Regulation of Television

- The original justification for the regulation of broadcasting by the federal government was decided in the 1969 Supreme Court case *Red Lion Broadcasting Co. v. FCC.*
- On October 3, 2004, NASCAR driver Dale Earnhardt Jr. was fined ten thousand dollars for using profanity on live television.
- In 2005, the Federal Communications Commission proposed $7.9 million in fines against the broadcasting industry, the most of any year in history.
- On June 15, 2006, President George W. Bush signed legislation increasing the amount of fines the FCC can levy on broadcasters who break decency regulations, up to $325,000 per incident.
- According to the Kaiser Family Foundation, 52 percent of par-

ents would like to see government regulation extended to cable television stations.

- According to a 2005 Harris Interactive poll, 53 percent of Americans surveyed said that the FCC was doing a poor job of upholding decency standards; 33 percent said the FCC was doing a "very poor" job.

Glossary

Censorship: Deleting content of print, performances, or broadcasts that is found objectionable, usually by a government body.

Deceptive: Deliberately causing one to believe what is not true or to fail to believe what is true.

Federal Communications Commission (FCC): An agency of the United States government that regulates all television and radio broadcasting in the nation, as well as national and international telecommunications.

Free market: An economic market in which supply and demand are either unregulated or subject to only minor regulations.

Indecency: The state of being immodest or unseemly, offensive to accepted standards of good taste or to public moral values.

Literacy: Having knowledge in a particular area; usually refers to reading and writing but can also refer to culture.

Obesity: The state of being very fat or overweight.

Obscene: Offensive to common morality or decency; arousing lust.

Prejudice: Unreasonable hostile feelings or attitudes, especially as relates to racial, religious, or national groups; irrational suspicion or hatred of a particular group.

Saturation: To be completely soaked or full of something.

Stereotype: A conventional, oversimplified conception, idea, or image.

Organizations to Contact

Alliance for Community Media
666 Eleventh St. NW, Washington, DC 20001
(202) 393-2650
fax: (202) 393-2653
Web site: www.alliancecm.org
The Alliance for Community Media is a grassroots organization that works to assure every citizen's access to electronic media. The alliance represents public access groups and community media centers throughout the country and works to advance its goals through government lobbying and public awareness and education. The group publishes how-to manuals for local community access producers, directories, and a regularly updated list of controversial programming.

American Civil Liberties Union (ACLU)
132 W. Forty-third St., New York, NY 10036
(212) 944-9800
fax: (212) 359-5290
Web site: www.aclu.org
The ACLU is the nation's oldest and largest civil liberties organization. It provides legal defense, research, and education and publishes the monthly newsletter *Civil Liberties Alert*, as well as pamphlets, books, and position papers.

American Decency Association
PO Box 202, Fremont, MI 29412
(231) 924-4050
fax: (231) 924-1966
e-mail: info@americandecency.org
Web site: www.americandecency.org
The American Decency Association is a nonprofit organization based on Christian principles and dedicated to combating obscene and indecent standards in the popular media, including television, through public education and advocacy, including demonstrations.

The group publishes a newsletter, *Frontline*, as well as regular bulletins and updates on its Web site.

Cato Institute

1000 Massachusetts Ave. NW, Washington, DC 20001
(202) 842-0200
fax: (202) 842-3490
Web site: www.cato.org

The Cato Institute is a nonprofit public policy research foundation that works to uphold libertarian principles, including limited government, individual liberty, and the free capitalist market. The institute opposes government regulation of media, including television. The institute publishes numerous resources, including policy papers, monographs, the monthly magazine *Regulation,* and the bimonthly newsletter *Cato Policy Report.*

Center for Media and Public Affairs

2100 L St. NW, Washington, DC 20037
(202) 223-2942
fax: (202) 872-4014
e-mail: mail@cmpa.com
Web site: www.cmpa.com

The Center for Media and Public Affairs is a research and education organization that conducts scientific studies of the news and entertainment media in order to provide an objective basis for debates over media bias and fairness. In addition to studies and monographs, the group also publishes books such as *Peepshow: Politics and Media in an Age of Scandal.*

Ethics and Public Policy Center (EPPC)

1015 Fifteenth St. NW, Suite 900, Washington, DC 20005
(202) 682-1200
fax: (202) 408-0632
e-mail: ethics@eppc.org
Web site: www.eppc.org

The Ethics and Public Policy Center is a think tank that works to apply the Judeo-Christian moral tradition to issues of public policy, including censorship and the media. The EPPC provides experts and scholars to the media and research resources for scholars. The center publishes numerous books and articles by its members.

Family Research Council
801 G St. NW, Washington, DC 20001
(202) 393-2100
fax: (202) 393-2134
Web site: www.frc.org
The council seeks to promote and protect the interests of the traditional family. It focuses on issues such as parental autonomy and responsibility, community support for single parents, and protecting children from inappropriate images in the media. The FRC publishes policy papers, position statements, and books such as *The ACLU vs. America: Exposing the Agenda to Redefine Moral Values*.

First Amendment Center
1101 Wilson Blvd., Arlington, VA 22209
(703) 528-0800
fax: (703) 284-2879
e-mail: info@fac.org
Web site: www.firstamendmentcenter.org
The First Amendment Center works to protect First Amendment rights through information and education, including freedom of speech and freedom of information. The center provides extensive research resources at its offices in Arlington, Virginia, and Nashville, Tennessee, as well as online. The center publishes the yearly report *The State of the First Amendment*, as well as guest editorials, pamphlets, and educational resources.

Focus on the Family
8605 Explorer Dr., Colorado Springs, CO 80920
(719) 531-3400
fax: (719) 531-3424
Web site: www.family.org
Focus on the Family is a Christian organization dedicated to preserving and strengthening the traditional family. Focus on the Family is concerned with decency standards on television and in other media and supports government controls and parental supervision. Focus on

the Family publishes numerous articles on its Web site, such as "Advice for the Modern-Day Family."

Media Awareness Network
1500 Merivale Rd., Ottawa, ON, Canada K2E 6Z 5
(613) 224-7721
fax: (613) 224-1958
e-mail: info@media-awareness.ca
Web site: www.media-awareness.ca
This organization is dedicated to promoting media literacy throughout Canada and the world. The group focuses on helping youth and their families place current media options in an educationally literate context and make informed media decisions. The group publishes educational kits for parents, teachers, and schools such as *Exploring Media and Race.*

Morality in Media
475 Riverside Dr., Suite 239, New York, NY 10115
(212) 870-3222
fax: (212) 870-2765
e-mail: mim@moralityinmedia.org
Web site: www.moralityinmedia.org
Morality in Media is a nonprofit corporation that works to combat obscenity and uphold decency standards on television and in other media. The group provides information on its Web site, as well as maintaining the National Obscenity Law Center, a clearinghouse of legal materials on obscenity law. Morality in Media publishes the *Morality in Media Newsletter* as well as two online monthly columns for parents.

Parents Television Council
707 Wilshire Blvd., #2075, Los Angeles, CA 90017
(213) 629-9255
fax: (213) 629-9254
Web site: www.parentstv.org
The Parents Television Council is a national grassroots organization that works against the presence of sex, violence, and profanity on television and in other media. The socially conservative group supports

government regulation of television and works with elected officials to uphold current broadcast decency standards. The council publishes a blog, Culture Watch, and regular articles and reviews for parents on its Web site as well as a newsletter, the *PTC Insider*.

For Further Reading

Books

Albert Abramson, *The History of Television, 1942 to 2000.* Jefferson, NC: McFarland, 2003. Written by a former CBS editor and cameraman, this book focuses on major television events in the post–World War II era of the twentieth century.

Eric Alterman, *What Liberal Media? The Truth About Bias and the News.* New York: Basic Books, 2003. A refutation of charges that the media are liberally biased. The author argues that such claims are blocking the public's full understanding of the news.

Ben H. Bagdikian, *The New Media Monopoly.* Boston: Beacon, 2004. A warning against the dangers of corporate media ownership.

Chas Critcher, *Moral Panics and the Media.* Berkshire, UK: Open University Press, 2003. An exploration of the media's role in sudden concern about moral issues in society.

D. Kirk Davidson, *Selling Sin: The Marketing of Socially Unacceptable Products.* Westport, CT: Praeger, 2003. A discussion of the methods used by those who sell products such as alcohol and cigarettes.

Murray Dry, *Civil Peace and the Quest for Truth: The First Amendment Freedoms in Political Philosophy and American Constitutionalism.* Lanham, MD: Lexington, 2004. A discussion of the Supreme Court's treatment of the First Amendment rights of freedom of speech and religion.

Marjorie Heins, *Not in Front of the Children: "Indecency," Censorship and the Innocence of Youth.* New York: Hill and Wang, 2002. An argument against current ideas about protecting children from supposed sexual material in the media.

Annette Hill, *Reality TV.* Oxford, UK: Routledge, 2005. An exploration into the purposes of reality television and ethical issues surrounding programming.

Robert L. Hilliard and Michael C. Keith, *Dirty Discourse: Sex and Indecency in Broadcasting.* Boston: Blackwell, 2006. An objective overview of sexual material on television and the radio, including an exploration of the shift in the definition of "sexual" as the demographics of America change.

Michele Hilmes, ed., *The Television History Book.* London: British Film Institute, 2004. A discussion of the influence a half-century of television broadcasting has had over social, cultural, and economic practices in Great Britain and the United States.

Su Holmes, *Understanding Reality Television.* Oxford, UK: Routledge, 2004. A collection of essays discussing reality television's influence on society and culture, including the history of early reality television.

Henry Jenkins, *Convergence Culture: Where Old and New Media Collide.* New York: New York University Press, 2006. Explains the author's thesis that new forms of media will interact with, rather than make obsolete, old forms.

Douglas Kellner, *Media Spectacle.* Oxford, UK: Routledge, 2003. A critical book discussing modern society's desire to put emotions and problems on public display.

Frederick S. Lane, *The Decency Wars: The Campaign to Cleanse American Culture.* Amherst, NY: Prometheus, 2006. A history of modern America's relationship with "decency," and the attempts to enforce it.

Robert W. McChesney, *The Problem of the Media: U.S. Communications Politics in the Twenty-first Century.* New York: Monthly Review Press, 2004. This book explores the biggest issues troubling American media, including bias, weak public broadcasting, and the quality of journalism.

Jason Mittell, *Genre and Television.* Oxford, UK: Routledge, 2004. The author proposes a method for understanding modern culture by exploring popular television shows and the categories into which they fall.

Shelly Palmer, *Television Disrupted: The Transition from Network to Networked TV.* Burlington, MA: Focal, 2006. A discussion of the issues affecting the television business in the twenty-first century.

Lynn Spigel and Jan Olsson, eds., *Television After TV: Essays on a Medium in Transition.* Durham, NC: Duke University Press, 2004. An overview of the present state of global television and predictions for the future, including discussions of TiVo, the rise of reality TV, and the influence of the Internet.

L.W. Sumner, *The Hateful and the Obscene: Studies in the Limits of Free Expression.* Buffalo, NY: University of Toronto Press, 2004. A discussion of the Canadian courts' methods of protecting free speech, including obscenity.

Periodicals

Katy Bachman, "CBS, Fox: FCC Indecency Policy Hurts Free Speech," *Mediaweek,* November 27, 2006.

Brooks Barnes, "New Deals Aim to Put the TV into Internet TV," *Wall Street Journal,* January 8, 2007.

Robert J. Barro, "The Liberal Media: It's No Myth," *BusinessWeek,* June 14, 2004.

Susan S. Bartell, "Thin Gruel for TV Viewers," *Newsday,* August 22, 2005.

William F. Buckley Jr., "The Search for Decency," *National Review,* May 22, 2006.

Chicago Sun-Times, "A la Carte Cable Could Be Death Knell for TV Diversity," September 17, 2004.

Drew Clarke, "In Reversal, FCC Says Consumers Save Under a la Carte," *CongressDaily,* February 9, 2006.

Danny Duncan Collum, "This Ad Is Your Ad," *Sojourners,* February 2007.

Geoff Colvin, "TV Is Dying? Long Live TV!" *Fortune,* February 5, 2007.

Michael Crowley, "Pay It Forward," *New Republic,* January 22, 2007.

Raymond L. Fischer, "Indecent Exposure," *USA Today* (magazine), May 2006.

Gazette (Montreal), "You Can Swap Houses, but Not Family Values," February 13, 2005.

Doug Halonen, "Media Ownership Crusade," *TVWeek,* June 5, 2006.

Omar Jabara, "The Vast Wasteland of Television News," *Denver Post,* April 3, 2005.

Derrick Z. Jackson, "A March on Too Much Television," *Boston Globe,* November 2, 2005.

David D. Kirkpatrick, "Feeding Frenzy for a Big Story, Even If It's False," *New York Times,* January 29, 2007.

Jemma Lewis, "I Have Given Up Watching Television," *Independent* (London), December 23, 2006.

Michael Murphy, "Desire for American Fare Never Greater Overseas," *TVWeek,* January 8, 2007.

Nation, "The War on al Jazeera," December 19, 2005.

New York Times, "F.C.C. Rules on Indecency," November 8, 2006.

Omaha (NE) World-Herald, "A Welcome Wearing Thin," May 16, 2005.

Pittsburgh Post-Gazette, "Keeping TV Under Our Thumb," September 5, 2004.

Pittsburgh Post-Gazette, "Must-Not-See TV," December 3, 2004.

William Powers, "As You Like It," *National Journal,* April 22, 2006.

David Reinhard, "Race-Based Survivor," *Portland Oregonian,* August 31, 2006.

Dorothy Rich, "Leave Your Televisions at Home," *Gazette* (Montreal), June 28, 2004.

John Robson, "Television Has Ruined Our. . .You Know. . .um . . . Whatever," *Ottawa (ON) Citizen,* September 8, 2004.

Howard Rosenberg, "Pain, Suffering, Prime Time," *Broadcasting and Cable,* November 29, 2004.

Steve Rosenbush, "Why the New FCC Rules May Bring Lawsuits," *BusinessWeek Online,* December 21, 2006.

Slate, "Fair and Balanced?" November 15, 2006.

Andreas Whittam Smith, "Why the Internet Makes Television News a Turn-Off," *Independent* (London), December 4, 2006.

Steve Sternberg, "Traditional TV: The Next Big Thing," *Mediaweek,* September 18, 2006.

Jesse Walker, "Muddy Rules," *Reason,* February 2007.

Edward Wyatt, "Next Project for Oprah: Feel-Good Reality TV," *New York Times,* December 16, 2006.

Mortimer B. Zuckerman, "The Tyranny of Imagery," *U.S. News & World Report,* October 30, 2006.

Mortimer B. Zuckerman, "Why TV Holds Us Hostage," *U.S. News & World Report,* February 28, 2005.

Web Sites

Common Sense Media (www.commonsensemedia.org). This group promotes reasoned solutions to the problem of media saturation for children. The site includes extensive resources for parents who want to limit their children's exposure to media, including an online newsletter, a blog, a resource bank, and reviews of current television shows and movies.

Federal Communications Commission (www.fcc.gov). The Web site of the federal agency includes a searchable database of all broadcasting rules and regulations, records of its hearings, fact sheets, and a help center for parents.

Media Freedom Project (www.mediafreedomproject.org). This project of the group Americans for Tax Reform advocates free-market solutions for media, technology, and telecommunications. The site includes letters the project has sent to lawmakers and information for those who wish to join.

National Institute on Media and the Family (www.mediafamily.org). This nonprofit organization is in favor of limited, regulated media for children, but not censorship. The group encourages parents to watch television with their children in order to help them understand content. The site includes fact sheets, education kits for parents and teachers, online columns, and an e-newsletter.

TV Watch (www.kintera.org). This coalition of various organizations opposes government regulation of television and advocates personal responsibility and parental controls instead. The site maintains a blog, tool kit for parents, and a list of shows that have been censored by the FCC.

Index

ABC, 60, 69, 72, 74

ACLU vs. America: Exposing the Agenda to Redefine Moral Values, 103

Advertisers, advertising, 11, 26, 31–34, 72, 76–78, 97

Advertising and Children, 76

A&E, 71

African Americans, 11, 23, 95, 98

Alcohol, 32, 77, 97

ALF, 40

Alliance for Community Media, 101

American
activities, 20–23, 45, 52–55, 97
attitudes, 10, 47–48, 93

American Academy of Pediatrics, 14, 16, 97

American Candidate, 71

American Casino, 71

American Civil Liberties Union (ACLU), 65–66, 101

American Decency Association, 10, 101

American Family, An, 70

American Psychological Association (APA), 15, 32, 75, 78, 97

Americus, GA, 60

Amusing Ourselves to Death: Public Discourse in the Age of Show Business (Postman), 55

The Apprentice, 64

Autism Speaks, 63–65

Bain-Selbo, Eric, 65

Baird, John Logic, 97

Baltimore City Paper, 58

Barton, Sen. Joe, 45

Behavior, 15–16, 26, 48

Berman, Gail, 88

Better Business Bureaus, 34

Bhutan, 97

Big Brother, 71, 88

Blogs, bloggers, 45

Bono, 69

Books, literature, 14

Boredom, 18

Boston, 26

Boston College, 60

Boston University, 77

Bozell, Brent T., 10

Brain development, 15–16

Bravo, 71, 88–89

Bridezillas, 71

Britain, British, 59, 97

Broadcast Indecency Enforcement Act, 11

Broadcasters, broadcasting, 10, 38–41, 43–46, 85, 88

Brownback, Sen. Sam, 44

Buck, Nina, 56

Bureaucracy, bureaucrats, 55, 82

Bush, George W., 10, 23, 98

Business Publishers, Inc., 58

Cable
choices, 10–11, 42–46, 52–53, 66, 68, 72, 85
networks, 81, 86–91, 93–96, 99

California, 62–64

Cancer, 53
Capitol Hill, 43
Cartoons, 55
The Casino, 71
Cato Institute, 10, 79, 102
CBS, 39, 71, 74
Celebrity, 49
Censorship, 9, 37–41, 43–46, 82, 85–86
Center for Media and Public Affairs, 102
Center for the Study of Popular Television, 61–62
Center on Children Families and the Law, 76
Center on Wealth and Philanthropy, 60
Centers for Disease Control and Prevention (CDC), 77
Charity, 47–49, 58–63, 65–66
Children
    impact, 25–28, 55–56, 61, 76–78, 81–85, 97–98
    influence, 9, 11, 13–19, 30–34, 37, 39, 45
Children's Advertising Review Unit [CARU], 34
Children's Tumor Foundation, 61
Christian Science Monitor, 97
Chronicle of Philanthropy, 58
Civil liberties, 10, 95
Civil Liberties Alert, 101
CNN, 21
Cognition, 16, 76
Colorado, 74, 78
Comcast Corporation, 92–93
Comedy, 55, 82
Comedy Central, 49
Commercials, 11, 30, 55
Computers, 15
Concerned Women for America, 86

Conservatives, 11, 37, 86
Consumers, customers, 11, 30, 34, 86–88, 90–91, 93–96
Consumers Union, 90
Content, 74–78
"Cops", 23
Corburn, Sen. Tom, 21
Crowley, Sheila, 62
CSI, 82
Culture, 48, 52, 54
Culture and Media Institute (CMI), 47–48
Culture Watch, 105

Dana, Charles A., 7
D.C. Central Kitchen, 65
Deadwood, 46
Decency, 10, 37–39, 86–88, 91, 98–101, 103–108
Denver, 75
Discovery Channel, 71
Diversity, 7, 54, 92, 95, 108
DVD, 60

Earnhardt, Dale Jr., 98
Economy, economics, 27, 60, 63, 93–95, 107
Education, 16–17, 28, 41, 58, 65–66, 78, 101–104
Egger, Robert, 66
Endemol USA, 62
ER, 82
ESPN, 88
Ethics and Public Policy Center (EPPC), 102–103
Everybody Loves Raymond, 24
Extreme Makeover: Home Edition, 60–63, 65–66

Fallujah, 23
Family, 13–15, 19, 34, 38, 65, 86
Family Guy, 49

Family Research Council, 37, 103
Family Television and
    Consultation Center, 18
Family values, 10–11
Fast food. *See* Junk food
Fastlane, 88
Fear Factor, 88
Federal Communications
    Commission (FCC)
    oversight, 32, 37–41, 44, 46,
        54, 69, 98–99
    regulations, 9–11, 77, 82,
        87–90
Federal Trade Commission
    (FTC), 32, 34
First Amendment, 45, 85, 103
First Amendment Center, 10
Flipper, 53
Focus on the Family, 103–104
Founding Fathers, 24
Fouts, Gregory, 97
Fox network, 49, 71, 88
Free market, 79, 86, 88, 91–92,
    110
Free-speech, 9–10, 30, 34
FX, 88

Game shows, 70
Gannett News, 88
Gerberding, Julie, 77
Gibson, Mel, 83
God, 48–49
Google, 21
Government
    censorship, 43–46, 79–82,
        85–86
    regulation, 9–11, 22, 51, 76,
        82–83, 92, 98–99, 102–103
    restrictions, 33, 39, 48–49, 73,
        85–86, 105, 110
Grassley, Sen. Charles, 21
Greenfield, Jeff, 21

Gross domestic product, 55
Growing Up Gotti, 71
Gulf of Mexico, 53

Habitat for Humanity, 60–61
Habits, 18, 26–28, 30–32, 48,
    53, 77, 85
The Hamptons, 69
Harris Interactive poll, 99
Harvard School of Public Health,
    25
HBO, 69
Health, 11, 15
Hispanics, 11, 95, 98
Hobbies, 18–19
Hollywood, 40, 49–50, 65
Homosexuality, 48
Hours of viewing, 9, 16, *22*
Hurricane Katrina, 20, 22–23

Illness, 14
Imagination, 13, 16–18
Indecency
    and censorship, 37–41, 43–46,
        80
    implications, 10–11, 76,
        85–86, 88–89
Inspiration, 53–54, 60
Intellectuals, 55
Internet, 7, 9, 66, 98
Iowa, 21
Iraq, Iraqis, 23

Jackson, Janet, 69, 82
Joe Schmo, 71
Journal of Broadcasting, 16
Journalists, journalism, 7, 45, 74
Judiciary Committee, 20
Junk food, 11, 21, 25–28, 33, 35,
    71

Kaiser Family Foundation, 32, 97–98
Kant, Immanuel, 56
Kelley, David E., 71
Kierkegaard, Soren, 56
Kimmelman, Gene, 90
Kleder, Martha, 86–91
Knight Center for Science and Medical Journalism, 77

Language, 13, 16–18, 37
Laws, 93
Lawsuits, 62–63
Lebanon Valley College, 65
Liberal, 52
Libertarianism, 9–10, 79
Lieberman, Sen. Joseph, 32
Lobbyists, 22, 38
Los Angeles Times, 15, 68

Mainstream vs. FTC, 32
Marketing. *See* Advertisements, advertising
Martin, Kevin, 40
Media, 9–11, 47–50, 82–84, 93
The Media Assault on American Values, 47–48
Media Awareness Network, 10, 98, 104
Merriam-Webster Dictionary, 38
Mill, John Stuart, 8
Minow, Newton, 54–55
Moore, Michael, 48
Morality in Media, 104
Morals, morality, 47–50, 52–56
MTV, 63, 88, 91
Murder, 55
My Super Sweet 16, 21

Narcissism, 49
Nascar, 59, 98
Nascar Angels, 63

National Association of Broadcasters (NAB), 11, 39, 45
National Cultural Values Survey, 48
National Low Income Housing Coalition, 62
NBC/Universal, 59, 65, 71, 74, 89
Networks. *See also* individual networks, 15, 26
New Jersey, 61
New Orleans, 23
New York, 24, 53, 61, 63–65
New York Times, 53. 56, 59, 108, 109
News, 9, 22–23
Newspapers, 7, 45
Newsweek, 20
Nielsen Media Research, 98
Nip/Tuck, 85

Obesity, 11, 25–28, 30–34, 52, 55, 77
Omaha World-Herald, 9
Orfanakos, George T., 60
Outdoor activities, 15

Parents
  oversight, 9, 11, 15, 18, 26, 31–33, 39, 96
  responsibility, 45–46, 79–85
Parents Television Council, 10, 76, 104
The Passion of the Christ, 83
Paulson, Ken, 10
Peepshow: Politics and Media in an Age of Scandal, 102
Pew Research Center, 98
Philadelphia, 24
Philanthropy, 60, 62
Pimp My Ride, 63
Please Be Ad-vised: The Legal Guide for the Advertising Executive, 30

Politics, politicians, 20, 45
Postman, Neil, 55
Presidency, 10, 20, 22–23, 98
Prime-time, 82
Problem solving, 15
Programming, 21–22, 33
PTC Insider, 105
Public, 10, 45, 55
Pulitzer Prize, 68

Queen for a Day, 60
Queer Eye for the Straight Guy, 89
Quiz shows. *See* Game shows

Reality shows, 58–59, 68–72
Reason, 42, 52
Red Lion Broadcasting Co. v. FCC, 98
Regulation, 9–11, 51, 76–77, 82–83, 92, 98, 102–105
Regulation, 102
Religion, 49–50
Responsibility, 48–49, 79–85
Rhode Island, 24
Roberts, John, 21

San Francisco, 65
Sarah Silverman Program, 49
Satcher, David, 15
Satellite, 42–46, 85, 90. 93, 95
Schervish, Paul G., 60
Schutjer, Clifford, 7
The Secret Millionaire, 59
Sedentary behavior, 25–26
Sensationalism, 15
Sex, 9–10, 15, 37–38, 49, 52, 55, 88
Shell, Ellen Ruppert, 77
The Shield, 85, 88
Showtime, 69, 71
Sierra Club, 65
Simpson, O. J., 71

The Simpsons, 56
60 Minutes, 69
Smoking, 53, 97
Social Ills, 65, 78
Social Services, 65–66
Society, 11, 65–66, 79
Spike TV, 71
The Sopranos, 46, 85
Sports, 88
State of the First Amendment, 103
Stern, Howard, 69
Stevens, Sen. Ted, 39, 45
Straniero, Kathryn A., 60
Super Bowl, 82
Superior Court of Los Angeles County, 62
Survivor, 69–71
Syracuse University, 62

Talk shows, 59
TBS, 69
Technology, 21, 42
Teenagers, 21, 34, 39, 52, 55, 98
The Television Project, 21, 97
Thirteen Colonies, 24
Thomas, Danny, 53
Thompson, Robert J., 61–62
Three Stooges, 82
Tinley Park, IL, 60
Tobacco, 32
Together We Cope, 60
Trump, Donald, 64
TV Watch, 10
Type II diabetes, 77

U.S. Congress, 10, 20, 22, 32, 39–40, 45, 81–82
U.S. Department of Education, 17
U.S. Senate, 21, 39, 44, 82, 85, 92
U.S. Supreme Court, 21, 38–40, 45–46, 98
U.S. Surgeon General, 15

U.S. 10th Circuit Court of
    Appeals, 32
Ultimate Love Test, 72
University of Colorado, 74, 77
University of Nebraska, 76
University of Pennsylvania, 15

Valenti, Jack, 38–39
Values, 47, 49–50, 86
V-chip, 46, 85
Videos, 14–16, 27, 66, 77,
    81–83, 85, 90, 93, 96
Viewers
    activities, 63, 65–66, 68, 72,
        86–89, 92, 108
    patterns, 10, 13, 45, 47–49,
        56, 58–60, 87
Violence, 9–10, 13, 15–16, 52,
    55, 77–78, 81–84
Virginia, 24, 53

Voyeurism, 49

Wallace, Rusty, 63
Washington, D. C., 10, 20, 22,
    62, 66, 82
Watchdog organizations, 9
WE network, 71
Web sites, 8, 45, 65, 105
The West Wing, 56
Westerns, 55, 70, 81
White House, 77
Wilcox, Brian, 76
Winfrey, Oprah, 59
Wirthlin Worldwide, 88
Wiseman, Fred, 70
Without a Trace, 39
Worst-Case Scenario, 69

Yale University, 18

Picture Credits

Cover: Reproduced by photos.com
Ted Thai/Time & Life Pictures/Getty Images, 12
Carl D. Walsh/Aurora/Getty Images, 14
The White House/Getty Images, 23
AP Images, 28, 36, 40, 43, 54, 64, 73, 75, 83, 89
David H. Wells/Aurora/Getty Images, 31
Frederick M. Brown/Stringer/Getty Images, 50
Kevin Winter/Getty Images, 70
Arnaldo Magnani/Getty Images, 94